THE MILLS OF JARRAHDALE

A Century of Achievement

1872 - 1972

A History

V. G. Fall

Registered in Australia for transmission by post as a Book.

A catalogue record for this book is available from the National Library of Australia

First printing 1972.
Second printing 1979 by the sponsorship of Alcoa Australia, W.A. Operations.

Printed for the sponsors by
CM Advertising, Publishing, Claremont
and Scope Printing Services, Willetton.

Copyright © 2022 V. G. Fall
All rights reserved.
ISBN-13: 978-1-922727-23-7
Third Edition produced by:

Linellen Press
265 Boomerang Road
Oldbury, Western Australia
www.linellenpress.com.au

Preface

to the Second Edition

The first edition of the late V.G. Fall's "The Mills of Jarrahdale" marked the centenary of our town in 1972. It seems fitting that the second edition be reprinted in 1979, the sesqui-centenary of this State.

The Jarrahdale Parents and Citizens' Association wish to thank the late V.G. Fall and his family for their generosity in allowing the Association to benefit from the profit resulting from the book's sale.

Thanks, must also go to Alcoa Australia for making the second reprint possible by underwriting the cost of the books' production.

Boyd Meiers
On behalf of the People of Jarrahdale, 1979

By the same author:
The Sea and the Forest,
A History of the Port of Rockingham
(University of Western Australia Press)

Note. Some of the material contained in Part 2 of this work has been drawn from the Author's book, *The Sea, and the Forest*, published in 1972 by the University of Western Australia Press, of Nedlands, Western Australia.
All direct quotations from The Sea and the Forest are marked by footnotes throughout the present text.

Preface
to the Third Edition

This third edition of *The Mills of Jarrahdale* is reprinted to help mark the occasion of the 150th anniversary of our town.

It has been made possible with financial assistance from the Australian Museums and Galleries Association, by providing us with a grant through its Chart programme.

The Jarrahdale Heritage Society also wishes to thank the family of the author, the late V.G. Fall, for vesting copyright to the Society, allowing it to benefit from sales of the book.

Diana Henniker
President

Contents

Preface to the Second Edition iii
Preface to the Third Edition v
Contents vii
    Illustrations ix
Part 1 1
    Introduction 1
Part 2 10
    The Jarrahdale Story 10
Afterword 99
About the Author 101
Appendix 1 103
    The Many Mills of Jarrahdale 1872-1972 103
Appendix 2 107
    The Owners of Jarrahdale 1870-1972 107
Appendix 3 110
    Some Notable Careers 110
Appendix 4 115
    Local Government in the Serpentine Jarrahdale District 115
Notes and References 122
    Books and Documents Consulted 122

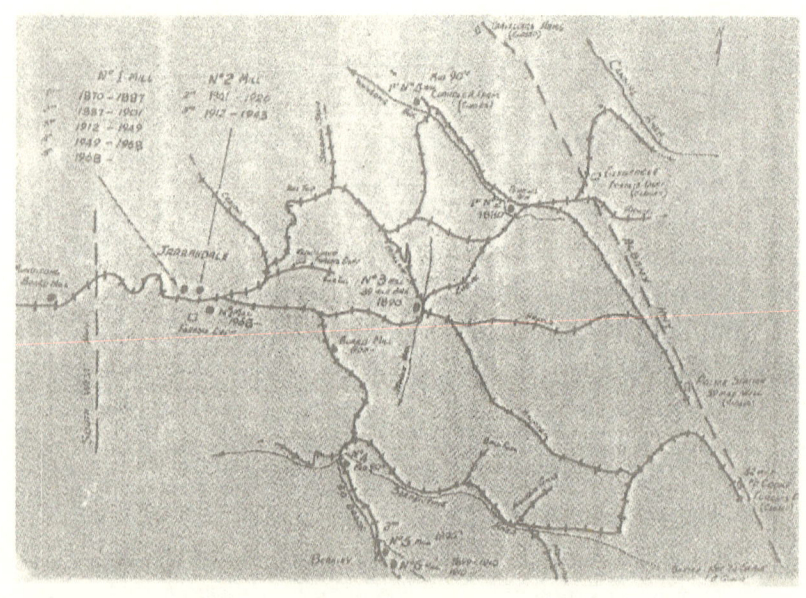

Map of Railway Lines and Mill Locations

Illustrations

No.		Page
1	Governor F. A. Weld, 1869-1874	8
2	Site of original Jarrahdale Mill of 1872	8
3	Locomotive's "Pioneer", "Samson No. 1" and "Samson No. 2"; 1890	9
4	Locomotive "Samson No. 1"; 1882	9
5	The "Millbrook Hotel", built c1888	29
6	Jarrahdale Junction (Mundijong) in 1899	29
7	Passenger coaches used on Rockingham-Jarrahdale Railway	30
8	No. 3 Mill ("The 39") c 1895	30
9	Head Office, "Rockingham Railway & Jarrah Forests Ltd." At Moore St., East Perth, 1892	36
10	Locomotive "Rockingham", at Jarrahdale c1900	37
11	Rockingham Jetties, 1895	37
12	Jarrahdale township, in 1890s	39
13	Log-hauling team and whim c1900	45
14	Mill Manager's house, Jarrahdale; built for Neil McNeil, 1889	46
15	Workers' houses at Jarrahdale in 1924	46
16	A "Bush Camp", early 1900's	47
17	A "Bush Log Landing", c1905	51
18	A Log Landing, with A. C. Munro, Manager of Jarrahdale, 1899	52
		52

19	The 'Murray Arms" Hotel, Jarrahdale, built c1894. The small building in middle distance is the first office of the original Jarrahdale Road Board, 1913	
20	The railway disaster of April 1901 (Loc. "Samson")	57
21	Mobile Bush School, Jarrahdale, 1920's	63
22	Henry Teesdale Smith, General Manager of Millars' Karri & Jarrah Co. Ltd. 1907	67
23	Joe Lewis, Mill Foreman, 1883 to 1926, with his sons c1914	69
24	"Cope's Boarding House", early 1900's	70
25	Mrs. Cope and her daughter Nellie Cope, early 1900's	70
26	Group outside Cope's Boarding House, 1898, James Cope (1824 to 1900) first on right in front row	71
27	The Big Strike. 8 Hours. Millars	78
28	"St George's House", St. George's Terrace, Perth, when built in 1913 as the Head Office of Millars Timber & Trading Co. Ltd	79
29	Jarrahdale-Rockingham excursion train, 1924	79
30	Alfred Cook, Manager of Jarrahdale 1935 to 1958. A photograph taken in 1969	84
31	The new sawmill of 1968	85
32	G. W. G. Watkins, Esq., Chairman of Serpentine Road Board, 1902	108
33	Council Chambers of the SJ Shire, at Mundijong, March 1972	108

NOTE: Illustrations Nos. 2, 3, 5, 6, 9, 11, 12, 14, 15, 16, 18 and 20 are reproduced from *"The Sea and the Forest"*, written by V. G. Fall and published by the University of Western Australia Press, 1972.

Part 1

Introduction

The Waiting Forest

From the first foundation in 1829 of the Swan River Colony, now the State of Western Australia, the early colonists were impressed, even overawed, by the vast forests which clothed the land for hundreds of miles around their early settlements.

As their exploring parties pushed inland to discover what sort of land they had come to inhabit they found that they were faced with "a succession of tree-covered mountains",[i] and in July 1830, within a year of the first landing, Ensign Dale, probing southwards from the infant settlement at Perth, reported that he ... "groped his way amid the jarrah forests" and that his party "pioneered their way among jarrah trees which grew to enormous heights and dimensions ... while ... some of the ridges ... were rendered glorious by those stately monarchs of the West Australian woodland – the jarrah".[ii]

Later in the same year – December 1830 – Captain Bannister crossed the Darling ranges and found ... "the usual fine jarrah, then called mahogany, surmounting summits or shading the glens".[iii] He found that the forest went on for mile after mile until the party was approaching King George's Sound when he reported that ... "The blue gums were of large dimensions; one measured 42 feet circumference and rising straight as a barrel of a gun to 140 or 150 feet before a branch was projected".[iv]

Wherever parties pushed out into the unknown they found ... "on every side ... woodlands extending to the horizon".[v]

It was at once realized by every settler, from Governor Stirling himself down to the humblest colonist who sought to clear a patch of land on which to build his home and sow his first crops, that the forest itself provided the greatest natural asset, and was there around him waiting to be exploited. For untold centuries, for millennia, the forests had awaited this moment, and now their time had come. Everywhere around the early settlements the pit-sawyer got to work, especially around the new-born city of Perth, where the jarrah grew thick and straight and tall. Some of the finest jarrah grew where Kings Park now stands, and here saw-pits were dug – traces of them can still be seen today – and the sound of axe and saw became familiar to the nearby settlers as more and more trees were felled to meet the ever-increasing demands of the growing town. All around Perth, wherever good jarrah stood, the sawpits went in and presently rows of houses stood where once the jarrah grew.

Apart from local needs, it was soon apparent that timber could provide a source of much-needed export income for the new colony and Governor Hutt (1839-46), who had taken over from Governor Stirling, soon pointed out that ... "The readiest means of employing what little capital they had was in their forest resources, and by a timber trade and by generally increasing exports they hoped to draw money into the colony".[vi] This was in 1844, and soon afterwards samples of various West Australian woods were sent to London, a small trial shipment being exported during the year, which sold for £10 a ton.

It was easy for an ambitious Governor and an enthusiastic

Press to point out the advantages to be gained from an export trade in timber, but to put these ideas into practice was a different matter altogether.

For the proposals to become a reality, three things were needed, skilled labour, ready access to a shipping port and above all, capital – much capital – and in the struggling colony of those early days all these essentials were lacking, especially the capital. It was also realized that for any big-scale production steam power was needed and it was some time before steam engines of any kind made their appearance in the colony.

Early Steam Sawmills

Probably the first of these mills was erected in 1833 at Mount Eliza, where good jarrah was found and where pit-sawing had been going on for the past three or four years. This pioneer mill was built by J. H. Monger, a colonist of 1829. This is probably the mill referred to by W. B. Kimberley in his "History of West Australia", published in 1897. Kimberley states that in 1837 "the Colony possessed ... a corn and sawmill and a powerful steam engine".[vii] However, a sawmill erected at Guildford in 1844[viii] is also claimed to be the first in the colony, while in the same year another mill was said to be in operation at Belmont.

Early water-powered mills

Here and there, and at a somewhat later period, small water-driven mills were built. Some of these were used for sawing timber, others for grinding flour. Little is known of them although the sites of several are still visible.

A notable one, used for sawing timber, was built by Buckingham at Roleystone in 1868, and was in use for many years; its site is now marked by a memorial cairn. There was another, believed to have been used for grinding flour, situated on the Serpentine River, about three miles from Jarrahdale. Here the old stone grinding wheels were still to be seen until recent years. It is said that the sandalwood carters, whose track passed nearby on the way to Rockingham, used to leave sacks of wheat at the watermill to be ground into flour, which they picked up on the return journey.

Thomas Peel's proposals

It was in the very early days – in the late 1830s and 1840s that Thomas Peel proposed to commence production for an export market, with timber sawn from the extensive tract of forest land which had been granted to him. Peel had initiated an ambitious scheme of colonisation and had brought to Western Australia some 500 settlers in three ships *"Gilmore"*, *"Hooghly"* and *"Rockingham" in 1829-30*. Peel considered using Safety Bay, which he called "Peel Harbour" as the place of shipment for his proposed exports but, like most of his schemes, the plan failed, largely through his own incapacity.

In 1845, Marshall Waller Clifton, the Chief Commissioner of the Australind company, which was attempting to establish a colonisation scheme near Bunbury, wrote to the British Admiralty proposing that a naval ship-building yard be established at Safety Bay, using the "West Australian Mahogany' which grew in profusion in the nearby hills.[ix] Nothing came of the proposal and shortly afterwards a survey of Safety Bay by the Surveyor-General, John Septimus Roe, showed that it was unsuitable for a harbour, and that Mangles Bay, further to the North in the sheltered waters of Cockburn Sound was much better for the purpose. This suggestion was quickly followed up by the founding of a township, named

Rockingham, after Peel's ship of that name which was wrecked in the area in May 1830. The Township was declared open for the purchase of town lots in 1847, and in the following year a tramway, or railway line was surveyed from the new township to the nearby hills. Even so, the township did not develop nor was a railway built until a generation had passed; indeed, the whole scheme of establishing a sawmill in the hills with a railway to a seaport, lapsed for some twenty-five years.

Other timber-milling ventures

Meanwhile, in other areas, some progress had been made. Benjamin Mason, who had a saw-pit station in the hills about five miles from the Canning River as early as 1864, later built a steam sawmill in the same district about 18 miles from Perth. Further south, in the Vasse (Busselton) area, Henry Yelverton who, like Mason, had started a pit-sawing establishment in the 1850s, later – in 1858 – also built a steam sawmill which was in the first mill of any size to work for any length of time.[x] Yelverton's' mill was about one and a half miles from the coast of Geographe Bay, at Quindalup, where a shipping jetty was constructed.

Throughout the 'Fifties and the 'Sixties, the timber industry remained primitive and small-scale, being much less important than the busy and profitable sandalwood trade which for most of the colony's early years brought in far more export income than did the native hardwoods.

The hardwood industry was waiting for some outside influence and above all for some outside capital before it could make any worthwhile advance. The outside influence came with the arrival in 1869 of Governor Weld.

Governor Sir Frederick Aloysius Weld

Weld arrived in September 1869 and held office until January 1875, during which period he did much to promote the interests and development of the colony, and indeed did so much to forward the production of the local hardwood timber industry he can justly be called "The Father of the West Australian Timber Industry."

He brought much experience of colonial problems with him, as he had been at one time Premier of New Zealand. During his time in Western Australia, he liberalised the form of Government, encouraged exploration and saw the establishment of the first electric telegraph (1869), the first railway, the first regular steamship communication with the Colony of South Australia and promoted the creation of a system of Local Government (1871).

"Weld was a devout Roman Catholic and the dedicated patriarch of a rapidly growing family. He was tall, slim, and erect, and his handsome face supported two bushes of Dundreary whiskers".[xi]

The new Governor lost no time in making himself personally familiar with the colony he had come to rule, and before the end of March 1870 had visited every settled area, covering, mainly on horseback, a distance of over 2000 miles.

During his journey he was particularly impressed by the extent and quality of the forests, noting that ... " ... Western Australia, as far as I have seen is covered with one vast forest". He determined that during his term of office an active timber industry should at last come into being. Weld soon realised that one of the factors which had delayed the establishment of any large-scale enterprise in this field was the lack of long-term security for investors, as hitherto sawmillers could only operate on short-term licenses. He proposed to solve this problem by replacing these licenses with long-term leases, or "Concessions", and did all he could to persuade the Home Government to agree to this proposed innovation, and to help to attract outside capital to invest in the production of West Australian timber.

His efforts met with considerable success; three separate schemes being put in hand within eighteen months of his arrival. These schemes were: -[xii]

1. The "West Australian Timber Company's" concession at Yoganup, with its sea jetty at Lockerville, near Busselton.
2. The "Canning Jarrah Timber Company's" concession originally held by Mason, Bird & Co., which shipped its timber down river from a landing on the Canning River.
3. "The Rockingham Jarrah Company's" concession at Jarrahdale, with its jetty at Rockingham.

Thus by 1870, thanks to Governor Weld, the ground had been prepared and the foundations laid for a mighty industry, which, after the passage of a hundred years, is still one of the mainstays of the State's prosperity, and no part of which has had a greater influence and effect than the early venture at Jarrahdale.

1. *Governor F. A. Weld, 1869-1874*

2. *P2003.001 Site of original Jarrahdale mill of 1872*

3 Locomotive's "Pioneer", "Samson No. 1" and "Samson No. 2", 1890

4 Locomotive "Samson No. 1" 1882

Part 2

The Jarrahdale Story

Beginnings

The new opportunities for investors in the Western Australian timber trade attracted the attention of a group of investors in the colony of Victoria, notably the brothers T. D. and Wm. Wanliss of Ballarat. T. D. Wanliss was a notable public figure, being the proprietor of the Ballarat Star and having interests in several gold mining companies. Associated with the Wanliss brothers was Peter Lalor, who in 1854 was the leading figure in the famous incident of the Eureka Stockade and who, in the following year, entered Victorian politics as the representative of Ballarat. Yet a third member of the group was James Service, another well-known citizen. This group formed a syndicate, on whose behalf Wm. Wanliss wrote a letter to the Western Australian Colonial Secretary, F. P. Barlee, dated 26th September 1870,[xiii] asking for a concession of 500,000 acres of forest land in the Cockburn Sound area.

Considerable negotiations followed, and eventually, after the approval of the Home Government had been obtained, a lease of 250,000 acres of prime jarrah forest was granted, with the proviso that a sawmill be constructed in the forest, that jetties be built in Mangles Bay (Rockingham) and that a railway be built to connect the sawmill with these jetties.[xiv]

The capital for this venture was subscribed mainly in the colony of Victoria, although a portion came from India and from Europe.

At last, all the ingredients for the start of a large-scale, well financed timber enterprise were present, and behind all this the hand of Governor Weld can be seen. Thus, Jarrahdale was born.

The original syndicate did not last long, a new company named "The Rockingham Jarrah Company" being formed in 1871.

The building of the first Sawmill

The new company got to work with a mill, and very soon machinery and equipment began arriving at Fremantle. In September 1871, a steam traction engine arrived, this being known as the "Thomson Road Steamer". This vehicle, a prodigy for those days, caused considerable debate in the local press, notably in the *Inquirer*, and some correspondents claiming that the "Steamer" would not be suitable for the rough work required of it, much of the argument being about the solid rubber tyres with which the tractor was equipped – quite a new thing at the time. The first use to which the "Thomson Steamer" was put was to bring 13 tons of flour from Fremantle to Perth, and this proposal again raised much debate, as many people thought that it would break down the bridge over the river.[xv] However, all went well, the flour was delivered, and the "Steamer" became a useful vehicle, taking heavy loads of machinery for the construction of the sawmill, and afterwards for hauling heavy loads of logs.

Meanwhile, an order had been placed as early as June 1870 with the Phoenix Foundry in Victoria for a locomotive, which arrived in sections at Fremantle in December 1871.[xvi] The new locomotive, the second to arrive in the colony (the first being imported by the "Western Australian Timber Company" for use on the Yoganup-Lockeville Line) was named the "Governor Weld", in honour of the Governor who had done so much to help the venture.

All the time the machinery for the mill itself was arriving, and as early as October 1871 Wanliss was advertising in the *Inquirer* ...

> *"Rockingham Jarrah Company"*
>
> *Tenders wanted for carting 40 or 50 tons of machinery from Mason's Landing to the Company's works at Jarrahdale, near Serpentine"* ...

signing himself, *"Wm. Wanliss, Superintendent."*

Even earlier than this, he had advertised for: -

> *"Six pairs of sawyers; also tenders for making twenty Navvy barrows."*

There was obviously no lack of efficient and energetic management, and before long the mass of machinery, including the sections of the locomotive, began to move from Fremantle on the long and difficult journey to Jarrahdale.[xvii]

The first part of the trip was easy, as the machinery was taken up the Swan and Canning rivers to Mason's Landing, a river wharf built by Mason, Bird & Co. for loading timber from their sawmill on to lighters to go down river to Perth and Fremantle. Here the machinery for Jarrahdale was transferred to wagons and the long overland haul began, along the Albany Road to a point about 36 miles from Fremantle, not far from where a sandalwood-carting track entered the forest. In this stretch the "Thomson Steamer" was a great help. Sir Hal. Colebatch, in his *"Story of a Hundred*

Years" records ... "The consternation of the blacks when the mill machinery was brought to the site, from a landing on the Canning River, by a traction engine, that being the only feasible method of carting the heavy loads. When the natives saw the engine puffing along with sparks flying out of the flue and steam out of the side, they ran away in great fright, declaring that it must be 'Jingey' – meaning the Devil"[xviii]

In spite of the immense difficulties the great task was accomplished, and throughout the second half of 1871 and well into 1872 the beautiful valley of the Cooralong resounded to the clang of hammers and the sound of saws, as with remarkable speed the mill took shape on the bank of the stream.

It was a well-chosen spot; the Wanliss brothers knew their business. Any sawmill needs a carefully chosen site. It must have plenty of pure water, so a dam was built in the Cooralong Creek, just up-stream from the mill. This dam still exists. The mill should be on gently sloping ground, so that the great jarrah logs as they are brought in from the bush, can be rolled down the log landing to the waiting saws on a sloping platform, which must not be too steep. The site of this log landing can still be seen. The site must have level ground on which the mill itself can be erected, and ample level ground around it to take the sawn timber as it emerges from the mill, loaded on "galloping-out" trollies, pushed by two strong workers, who ran it out to the stacking area. Finally, the mill must be as close as possible to the forest, or "bush", so that the haul from the bush to the mill is as short as possible – especially in the early days of operation. This haul must also be on a grade on which in due course a railway could be built, when the time came that the distance became too great for direct hauling by the log teams to the sawmill.[xix]

All the essentials were provided, either by nature or by man, on the Jarrahdale site, and about the forest, the finest area of jarrah in the whole colony was all around the new mill. It is an interesting fact that, eighty years later, in 1950, the fallers were working for the second, or maybe for the third time within sight and sound of the original mill of 1872.

Truly, the Wanliss brothers had chosen well.

So well, too, had the workers toiled that in May 1872, only some eight months after the start of the job, the mill was completed, and the saws, driven by steam, began to whine through the great logs ... a sound which has rarely ceased for a hundred years.

Not only had the mill been built, but other buildings had gone up: a workshop, a material store, and huts and some houses for the workers. A truly remarkable achievement.[xx]

The Jarrahdale-Rockingham Railway

All the time the sawmill was under construction the railway – or tramway – line was steadily going through to Rockingham. The first line was built of 4 x 3 jarrah, with "round-back" sleepers. The wooden rails were pegged down to the sleepers, and had iron reinforcing plates at the curves, which were kept well-greased, greasers usually working on the job daily.[xxi]

The distance covered was 23½ miles, 7 miles to what afterwards became "Jarrahdale Junction" (and later Mundijong) and 16½ miles from thence to the Rockingham jetty. The gauge was 3'6", which eventually became the standard gauge throughout the colony.

It was soon found that damage to the wooden rails was excessive so "Lowmore" iron strips were affixed to the top of the wooden rails to reduce wear. These were only a limited success, as they had the tendency to lift at the ends, so that every time a rake of trucks went down to Rockingham, a supply of wooden rails and iron strips was taken. There was a guard on every truck, and when derailment took place – which was often – it was the duty of the guards to jack the truck back onto the rails and, if necessary, to replace the broken wooden rail and the damaged iron strip. The track to Rockingham soon became littered on each side with broken rails and twisted iron strips.[xxii]

This was an expensive business, especially as the round trip, down to Rockingham, unload at the jetty and proceed back to Jarrahdale, took two to three days. As it was soon found that the weight of the locomotive – (even the little "Governor Weld" weighed eight tons) – caused great damage to the rails, the loaded timber trucks were towed by horse teams, the horses being unharnessed at the top of the hill, the loaded trucks being sent down, one by one, by gravity, being checked and controlled by a "whip" – a rope led through a single-sheaved block, anchored to a solid post, or tree, at the top of the hill.

On reaching the flat country at the foot of the slope the horses, which had been walked down the hill, were again harnessed, and towed the trucks past what is now Mundijong and Wellard to the jetty at Rockingham. Eight-horse teams were used and the provision of these, with the teamsters and the guards on the trucks, as well as the heavy maintenance costs of the line were a very heavy expense and probably was one of the causes of the lack of financial success of the original company and its immediate successors.

It was soon obvious that iron rails would have to be used, and another locomotive purchased if costs were to be cut down and profits made, and in due course these were provided, as will be later described.

The Jetties at Rockingham

The Railway was completed to the coast at Mangles Bay in November 1872 and just one month later, in December, the first deep-sea jetty was also completed. This jetty was 240 feet in length and had 28 feet of water at the end, being able to accommodate two vessels at once.[xxiii] As few ships of the period were over 500 tons, drawing less than 17 feet, there was ample water for any vessel likely to call for a timber cargo.

At the time there was no township at Mangles Bay, the "Rockingham" of the period being a small farming settlement at what is now known as "East Rockingham" – about 2½ miles inland on the "Fremantle – Mandurah Road. Here was a hotel – "The Rockingham Arms" – later known as the "Chesterfield Inn", a school and about a dozen houses. At Mangels Bay, the timber company therefore had to build a few huts for the workers who came down from Jarrahdale on the timber trains and who usually had to remain over at least one night. They also built huts for the storage of materials. Apart from this, there was nothing. The present town of Rockingham came much later, being brought into existence by the timber trade from Jarrahdale. Thus, Jarrahdale created Rockingham, the town on Mangles Bay, while gradually the original "East" Rockingham slowly ceased to exist.

The first ship to berth at the new jetty was the little 89-ton brigantine *"Northern Star"*, which came in January 1873, to load timber for Melbourne.[xxiv]

At this early period much of the timber brought down to the Rockingham jetty was loaded into lighters which took their loads to Fremantle or up the Swan River to Perth, for the local market, and this, too, was the way that most Jarrahdale people travelled when they went to the capital, although a mail cart did run about once a week, each way, from Fremantle to Mandurah, and on by the "Old Coast Road" to Bunbury.

Jarrahdale in the 1870's

A hundred years ago Jarrahdale was a small, crude, isolated township of around fifty houses and huts, with a population of around 300 or less. Jesse E. Hammond, in his interesting book of reminiscences, "Western Pioneers" was a witness of the operations at the mill in the very early 'seventies. He says:
_xxv

"At Jarrahdale I first saw a railway built, and an engine running on the rails, and the great rubber-wheeled traction engine pulling logs out of the forest. Some of the logs were 60 or 70 feet long and up to 7 and 8 feet in diameter. The only accident I saw was the breaking of the big chains that dragged the logs. If these chains held fast, the logs had to come when *that* engine was pulling. The sight of the saws going through the great logs was a thing few boys ever saw in their early days. It is hard to imagine that a huge tree standing half a mile, or a mile away from the mill in the morning could be seen stacked as sawn timber by nightfall. About halfway between Jarrahdale and Serpentine, a Mr. Batt, one of the oldest pioneers, lived with his two sons and two daughters. The sons were both employed at the mill with their bullock teams. Sometimes the two teams had to be "doubled-up" on a big log. This often happened when the traction engine was being used to put the logs in place at the mill."

This was Jarrahdale at the beginning; the mention of trees being felled in sight of the mill establishes the date – 1872 or at the latest 1873.

Even at the present day, when it has been cut over for a hundred years, the forest at Jarrahdale is an impressive sight.

A hundred years ago, before it had ever heard an axe or saw, it must have been magnificent. The great jarrah trees rose a hundred or a hundred and fifty feet to the sky, not in regular avenues or rows, but scattered; an enormous giant, perhaps sixty feet to the nearest limb, with a vast wide-spreading canopy of branches above, with a myriad of leaves shutting out the sun; there, three or four trees would stand in a group; in places were natural, park-like glades; everywhere the clean, pungent, aromatic scent of the eucalypt; underfoot a carpet of fallen green-brown leaves, interspersed with patches of green undergrowth. In spring, wildflowers were everywhere.

To newcomers, especially those who had but lately left the placid well-ordered scenery of the English Shires, with their small fields of lush green grass, bordered with trim, well-cared-for hedges, the grey-green immensity of the jarrah bush must have been awe-inspiring, indeed even terrifying. It was, and still is to this day, very easy to get lost in the bush, particularly when out of sight or sound of the mill. When one got a few hundred yards from the mill or mill township all evidence of human life vanished – there were no landmarks. Even those who had become somewhat accustomed to the bush had to proceed with caution, which in time became instinctive. The sun was their compass; if there was no sun then keeping a straight course was difficult indeed. The only tracks were those made by the big jinkers of the log-hauling teams, and these were no true guide, for they could well be old, leading to some long-abandoned logging site.

The workers in the mill rarely went into the bush unless it was their duty to do so, the possibility of getting lost was too great, especially in those very early days when habitations were few and widely scattered. For many years to come men would wander off from the mill township and get lost in the bush. Nearly always they were "new chums" who did not realise the risk. These unfortunates would lose their bearings when perhaps only a mile or two from the mill, which was all too easy to do, as the trees went on, without any landmark, for mile after mile, each area being exactly like the last. Often, they started going around and around in circles, not knowing that they were doing so. When they were missed by their mates, the mill whistle would be sounded to guide them home. If they had not found their way back by nightfall, they would have to stay in the bush all night, for to search in the blackness of the forest was out of the question, although parties would go out a certain distance, bearing lamps and calling out at the top their voices.

Truly, the bush was no place for fools.[xxvi]'

Early Post Office

When the mill first started there was no post office, the mail being handled by the sawmill office, the mail being sent down by a lad on horseback to the main Pinjarra-Armadale Road, where it was handed to the driver of the mail coach, the inwards mail bag being collected in the same way. Jesse Hammond recalls that his first job was given to him by Mr. Wicks, the secretary of the company, this being to act as mail man.[xxvii] Three of Hammond's brothers were working at Jarrahdale at that time.

A post and telegraph office were opened at Jarrahdale on 12th February 1880, a sign of the growing importance of the township.

Early Police Stations

When Jarrahdale mill and township were first built, and for many years afterwards, the only police station was the "Police

Post" on the Albany Road, not far from where the "36 mile" track from Jarrahdale joined the main road. This Post was also a changing station for the horses of the mail coaches, which ran regularly from Albany to Perth. The "Police Post" was in the charge of one constable with one aboriginal assistant. It controlled a wide district, including Jarrahdale when that centre came into existence; it also extended westwards as far as Rockingham at the time when that seaport was in its early stage of development.

Later, probably in the early 1880's, when Jarrahdale had grown into a substantial township, a police station was erected there with quarters which had formerly been a school, built by a retired shipmaster who had left the sea and set up a school at Jarrahdale.[xxviii] The first police station was practically opposite the Mill Brook Hotel.

Constable Bake was in there from 1916 to 1924, and Constable McGrath was there from 1927 to 1931 and then by Constable Rule who was in charge at Jarrahdale until 1934, when the police station was removed to Mundijong.[xxix] Constable (now Sergeant) Rule remained at Mundijong until 1938.

The Timber Company Changes Hands

The original Wanliss company had done good work. The sawmill was a success, the railway was functioning, and at the jetty the ships came and went. In 1873 seven vessels loaded about 1060 loads[1] of jarrah, in 1874 twelve ships lifted about

---

[1] A "Load" is a unit of measurement, consisting of 50 cubic feet or 360 superficial feet. For green jarrah, there are 360 super feet to the ton. In the West Australian timber trade quantities were (and still are) always expressed in loads, for quantities over 600 super feet: smaller quantities being expressed in super feet, i.e. 20 loads, 180 super feet.

3550 loads, not very impressive figures when it is realised that the mill could produce around 800 loads a month, or say 9000 loads a year, and had been built with a view to supplying a considerable export trade.

Soon the company was in financial difficulties; probably the scheme was, after all, a bit too ambitious; probably not enough work had been done on the marketing side. Whatever the cause, a new company, the "Rockingham Jarrah Timber Company" took over in 1874 and obtained a new timber concession for a term of 13 years, as from 1 January 1874. The new company had the advantage of a share in a tender submitted jointly with Mason Bird & Co. (Canning Sawmills) for 90,000 sleepers which was accepted by the South Australian Government Railways.

The "Pioneer" Locomotive

The new company realised that more haulage power was needed and at once purchased a new locomotive, which was built by the Fulton Foundry of Victoria in 1874. It was named the "Pioneer", and became a well-known sight, with its tall funnel belching black clouds of smoke as it puffed along the line to Rockingham with a rake of trucks in tow or shunted to and fro in the yards to Jarrahdale and Rockingham. It had a long life, as it was in constant use until 1904. The company now had two locomotives, the new "pioneer" and the "Governor Weld", as well as the traction engine, the famous "Thomson Steamer", which at about this time was converted to a locomotive running on rails and used for log-hauling from the bush to the mill.

However, the going was still hard, and in 1876 there was another change of ownership, but not of name, the *"Fremantle Herald"* reporting on 18 March 1876 that ... Mr. Hetherington representative of the new proprietors, arrived to take possession." There was an argument between William Wanliss and Hetherington on the matter of the ownership of the 80 acres of land on which the mill was built, Wanliss claiming that he, personally, had bought this from the Crown and had never transferred it to the outgoing company.

We do not know how the matter was settled, but there appears to have been a hold-up in production that year, and it is noted that there is no record of any ship loading at Rockingham in 1876.

A settlement of the dispute must have been arrived at before the year was out, as we find shipping in full swing again in 1877, when five vessels loaded about 2100 loads at Rockingham.

After this episode the company seems to have settled down to profitable trading and exports improved, nine ships lifting about 4400 loads in 1878, while a slightly larger quantity was shipped in 1879 and by 1880 exports were booming with at least 16 vessels loading jarrah and probably even more, as the shipping records for that year are incomplete.

Iron Rails

By this time the company realised that, if the railway was going to be efficient and profitable, the wooden rails would have to be replaced by iron. An order was therefore placed in England for a supply of these, and the first consignment arrived at Rockingham in the ship *"Gads Hill"* on 19 July 1878. To complete the job and to provide for extensions to the bush, a second shipment was ordered, which arrived in the barque *"Kilmeny"* in March 1882. Although both shipments were of light 30lb. rails they were a complete success, and they remained in use long after the seaport at Rockingham had gone out of use, not being pulled up until 1950, when the line from Mundijong was abandoned and the rails removed.

Jarrahdale in the 1880's

With the growing prosperity the sawmill was able to reach and maintain its full output, more workers were employed, and the township grew in size, and developed a lively social life of its own. Fortunately, we have a brief description of the life of the township in those days, written by Mrs. Phoebe Christie[2] Mrs. Christie writes:[xxx]

> *"In 1880 I lived at Jarrahdale, the mill having been opened in 1872. The timber at that time was carried to Rockingham by horse-drawn trucks over a wooden railway, and was shipped by the "Honour", under Captain Hughes and Captain Marilyer. Later the horse-drawn trucks were replaced by steam engines, the "Pioneer" and the "Samson". Jarrahdale at that time was thriving, and we had many and varied entertainments. There were weekly practices at the library of our "Glee Club", and we held concerts and dances. Mostly, the music was supplied by accordion or concertina. Picnics on the beach were also enjoyed. We travelled on the timber trucks."*

The timber vessel "Honor" (Not "Honour") was an Austrian barque of 577 tons. She was a frequent visitor to Rockingham in the 'Eighties.

The picnics on the beach, which Mrs. Christie refers to. were a feature of Jarrahdale life for over sixty years, the last one being held in 1943.

---

[2] "The memories of Mrs. Phoebe Christie", Journal of the W.A. Historical Society, Vol. IV. Part 2 1950

Jarrahdale Booms and Rockingham Becomes the Chief Timber Port of the Colony

By 1880 Jarrahdale was recognised as the leading timber station and Rockingham as the principal timber port of Western Australia.[xxxi] Twenty-five ships loaded in 1881 and no less than 30 in 1882, Rockingham port being fully recognised, well known and popular with shipowners, who now knew of its safe anchorages and good jetty facilities, being in this respect far ahead of Fremantle for safety and convenience.

The timber trade was booming. In the six years 1878-1883, the colony exported 92,000 loads of timber, an average of 16,000 loads per year, and of this quantity Jarrahdale, shipping through Rockingham accounted for more than one-half, this being equal to the combined total of timber shipped from all other mills and ports, including the new centre at Karridale, where the M. C. Davies Company had built their jetty at Hamelin Bay in 1882, to be followed later by a jetty at Flinders Bay. The Eastern Colonies – chiefly South Australia – took most of these exports, about 80,000 loads being shipped over East in these years, Jarrahdale providing more than half of it.

No. 2 Mill Is Built

It being during this period that the company, probably anticipating that the boom times would continue, built a second mill about twelve miles from Jarrahdale; this mill was abandoned about 1900, a replacement being built near the site of the original "No. 1" after the second mill was burnt down in 1901.

All this time the trade with Perth continued, lighters regularly sailing, or now more often being towed, from Rockingham to the Swan River with cargoes of Jarrahdale timber. However, the local trade with the metropolitan area was limited by the small size and slow increase of the population. In 1876 Perth had only 4,606 people and Fremantle 3,303, making a not very impressive total of 7,909, and this only increased very slightly in the next ten years. Indeed, it was not until the discovery of gold in the late '80s and particularly in the '90s that a real influx of population took place.

A Second Jetty Built – 1882[xxxii]

The increase in shipping had made it obvious that another jetty would soon be needed, and this was built in 1882 by David Law, the father of R. O. Law, who five years later obtained the contract for the final extension of Fremantle's "Long Jetty".

The "Samson No. 1" Locomotive[xxxiii]

In this year also yet another locomotive was purchased. This was the "Samson", the first of that name and therefore known as "Samson No. 1". It was built by Beyer, Peacock & Co. and proved to be a very useful engine. It had a distinctive "Balloon" chimney which made it easily recognisable. About 1895 this "Balloon" or "Diamond" chimney was altered to a tall "Stove Pipe" chimney. The loco worked all its life on the Jarrahdale-Rockingham railway and was a well-known sight for many years. "Samson No. 1" was sent to the Philippines in 1917 where the then owners of Jarrahdale (Millars Timber & Trading Co. Ltd.) had interests. The company then had three locomotives and two jetties, the latest one being 353 feet long, with 34 feet of water, and able to berth two large vessels; thus, four ships could be accommodated at once. All in all, the year 1882 was a busy and prosperous one for the Jarrahdale company.

In 1883 the timber trade of the colony declined, mainly because of the difficulty and cost of transporting sawn timber from the mills to the seaports, but in this Jarrahdale held a favourable position, and thus was well able to hold its own and in this year Jarrahdale despatched eighteen full cargoes of jarrah, a total of some 8,000 loads, but in the following year of 1884 the "Rockingham Jarrah Timber Company" felt the first breath of the depression in the industry, which continued for some years, exports from the colony falling from a peak of £93,650 in 1882 to £28,384 in 1887.

Jarrahdale was fortunate in sending away around 3,600 loads of jarrah in eight ships during 1884, although this increased to 6,600 loads sent in fifteen ships in 1885. That Jarrahdale was able to retain its pre-eminent position in these years can be seen from the following figures for timber cargoes exported in the four-year period 1882 – 1885: -xxxiv

Jarrahdale (via Rockingham)	65 ships
Lockeville	43
Karridale (via Hamelin)	32
Quindalup	<u>22</u>
	<u>162</u>

Thus, Jarrahdale produced and shipped 40% of the colony's total timber exports.

Proposed Railway Extension

It was during this busy period that the Jarrahdale company twice offered to extend the Rockingham-Jarrahdale railway line, in the first instance (1882) to the Albany Road, and in the second instance (1885) to connect with the new Perth to Albany line. Both offers were declined by the Government of the day; had they been accepted the result could well have been that Rockingham, and not Fremantle, would have become the chief port of the colony.

The next two years were difficult ones for the timber trade – even at Jarrahdale. Exports declined, only four, or possibly five vessels loading Jarrahdale timber in 1887.

Original Mill Burnt – 1895 xxxv

It was in these difficult circumstances that the company had the misfortune to lose its mill by fire. The manager, Mr. Ritchie, who had succeeded Mr. Steedman in the early 'eighties, was on leave, and a new young man A. C. Munro was brought over from Victoria to take charge. Munro, who had been born in Tasmania in 1858, was only 37 years old at the time. However, he knew his business thoroughly, young as he was, and rebuilt the mill, as the second No. 1 mill, without delay. The original mill had been constructed in the "American" style, being of two storeys. Munro built the new one in the more conventional single-storey design, and at the same time replaced the former circular 'breaking-down" saws with a vertical saw, which no doubt he considered more suitable to deal with the very large size logs which Jarrahdale was getting at that time from the still hardly touched and virgin bush.

At this period the Fremantle Long Jetty was completed, the timber for its construction being cut at Jarrahdale and lightered to Fremantle from Rockingham. The jetty was built by R. O. Law in partnership with Matthew Price. Later he was in partnership with William Atkins, who in 1888 was acting manager at Jarrahdale, after Munro had returned to Victoria.

Another Change of Ownership[xxxvi]

Probably owing to the difficulties of the preceding years, and no doubt owing to the need of more capital, the Jarrahdale company again changed hands. The new owners were "The Neil McNeil Company, Jarrahdale Timber Station", which was incorporated in Victoria in 1889, most of the capital coming from that colony. Other members of the organisation were Robert Reid, William McLean, J. Wittingam, and A. J. McNeil, the brother of Neil McNeil. At this time the timber concession was renewed for a period of 40 years, and thus did not expire until the last day of 1929, this being the last of the various timber concessions granted to any sawmiller on the lines first proposed by Governor Weld in 1870.

Another Locomotive – "Samson No. 2"[xxxvii]

The new company lost no time in obtaining another locomotive to add to their growing fleet. This engine was also built by Beyer, Peacock and was a replica of the successful engine supplied in 1882. It was called the "Samson No. 2". It also had the distinctive "Balloon" or "Diamond" smokestack, which however was altered to a "Stove Pipe" chimney, at the same time as was its sister-locomotive in 1895. At this time both locomotives were fitted with "Pick-up" injectors, enabling them to lift water from creeks and wells alongside the line. With the increasing length of the bush log line the locomotives had to carry greater quantities of water. Accordingly, Samson No. 1 (and possibly No. 2 also – authorities differ) was fitted with a large home-made steel water tank. In these years three locomotives were in regular use hauling logs from the bush to the mill and taking sawn timber down to Rockingham. The "Thomson Road Steamer" (afterwards a locomotive) had by this time disappeared from history, while the original engine, the little "Governor Weld", is believed to have been in use for shunting purposes only, mainly in the Rockingham yard and jetties.

5. P2003.175 The "Millbrook Hotel", built 1891

6. P2003.093 Jarrahdale Junction (Mundijong) in 1899.

7. P2013.015 Passenger coaches used on Rockingham-Jarrahdale Railway

8. P2003.040 No. 3 Mill ("The '39") c1985 203380P

The "Millbrook Hotel"

By the end of the 1880s Jarrahdale had become a solid and well-established community. It was now quite a town, with rows of cottages, good houses for the senior staff, churches, a store and – at last – a hotel, the "Millbrook Hotel", a wooden structure with wide verandah's, which stood on the left-hand side of the road from Jarrahdale Junction, just before the road crossed the Cooralong Brook on the old wooden bridge. The exact date of erection cannot be established, but the West Australian Directory for 1888 lists a J. J. Howe as a "Licensed Victualler" residing at Jarrahdale, so it is probable that the hotel was built at that date or possibly shortly before.

The advent of the hotel was not wholly welcomed by the mill manager, who complained of the ill effect of drink on his employees. Possibly the manager was Munro who was relieving manager in the year 1887. However, no doubt the employees welcomed it; after all, even at Jarrahdale there was not that much to do in the evenings.

Rockingham, the new seaport Rockingham on the coast, was growing, too. Some houses, real houses, had appeared to join the collection of sheds and workers' huts on the waterfront, and the timber yard had grown to a large size. A "General Store" had also been erected, and by 1890 a new hotel appeared at Rockingham also. This was the "Port Hotel", now the Rockingham Hotel. Thus Rockingham, as well as Jarrahdale, deserved the name of a "town".

The Wonderful 'Nineties

The Eighteen-Nineties ushered in the most remarkable period which the Colony of Western Australia had ever seen.

The gold discoveries of the late '80s paled into insignificance when compared with those which followed one another in quick succession during the following decade. The gold rush was on, and the population of the colony increased in leaps and bounds, the rise being from 42,137 in 1889 to 170,651 in 1899, while by 1903 Perth's population had risen to 46,400, a far cry from 4,600 of 1876 – tenfold increase.

This rapid increase in population greatly increased the need for houses, and more and more lighters towed up to Fremantle and on up the river to Perth, carrying Jarrahdale timber to a steadily growing market. At the same time exports remained at a high level, 7,100 loads from Jarrahdale being shipped during the year 1890 alone.

Another Change of Ownership

Probably the expanding market showed the need for more capital, as in March 1892, the company was re-organised, became the "Rockingham Railways and Jarrahdale Forests Company". The new company was incorporated in Victoria, as were the earlier companies. The year 1892 also saw the start of another undertaking, which although un-remarked at the time, was destined to have a profound effect on the future of Jarrahdale, and of its port at Rockingham. This was the start of work on the new Inner Harbour at Fremantle, the brainchild of that great engineer C. Y. O'Connor.

In the following year, 1893, Jarrahdale's best-known and most energetic manager was appointed.[xxxviii] This was A. C. (Alex) Munro who, as we have seen, had acted as temporary manager in 1887. It was under Munro's leadership, backed to the full by McNeil, that Jarrahdale was well and truly put on the industrial map of the colony. Munro left his mark, not only on Jarrahdale, but also on the whole of the timber industry in the West, in which he was a prominent figure for over forty years.

Jarrahdale Junction

It was in this busy year, when Munro had just taken over management, that another event took place which had an enormous influence on the future of Jarrahdale and of Rockingham. This was the completion of the new Bunbury-Perth government railway. This crossed the Jarrahdale-Rockingham line at a place later to be named "Jarrahdale Junction" and now called Mundijong. Here there was an "H" or "Diamond" crossing, the two sets of railway lines crossing each other at right-angles, thus making a "diamond" or an "H", a very rare and unusual arrangement.

One of the provisos made by the Jarrahdale company, when negotiating with the Government for the crossing, was that the timber company's trains had precedence over the Government trains in the use of the crossing – another most unusual arrangement. This right was retained right up to 1950, although it is not known how often it was exercised.[xxxix]

From this time onwards it was possible for the timber from Jarrahdale to be railed right through to Perth, and as a result the lighter trade from Rockingham came to an end. So heavy did the traffic become on this new line, as timber and other goods were being railed from stations all along the line, that the Government rolling stock could not cope with it. Accordingly, arrangements were made for the Jarrahdale company to run its own locomotives and rake of timber trucks on the new Government line from Jarrahdale Junction to Perth. It is pleasing to think of one of the balloon funnelled "Samsons" chuffing through the traffic yard of the Perth Central Station, with a load of Jarrahdale timber, stowed on the Jarrahdale company's own trucks!

New Sawmills

The 'Nineties were halcyon days for Jarrahdale. So great was the demand for timber, not only for local use but also for overseas, that no less than four new mills were built between 1893 and 1899[3],[xl]

All of these were some distance from the original "No. 1" mill and township. "No. 3" mill, usually known as the "39" was eight miles from old Jarrahdale, being on the "39 Brook", which flows into the Serpentine River. "No. 4" was also about eight miles from Jarrahdale, on the Serpentine River. "No. 5" mill was at "Jarrahglen", fifteen miles to the north-east of old Jarrahdale. It was known as "Chandler's" ... it was later rebuilt on Big Brook, ten miles to the south-west of Jarrahdale. "No.6" mill was built in 1899, being also on Big Brook. At all these mills small townships grew up; they even had their own schools.

By 1899 over 300 men were employed at the Jarrahdale station while 140 horses and 100 bullocks were continually at work.[xli] The railway ran from Rockingham through Jarrahdale and on into the bush, where the track was being constantly extended as the trees closer to the mill were cut out. Over its whole length, by the end of 1899, it was more than 60 miles long.

Two New Hotels – 1894

The growing prosperity stimulated further by the opening of the new South-west Railway in '93, led to the building of two hotels. The first of these was the "Murray Arms' hotel, which

---

[3] See appendix 1, "The many mills of Jarrahdale".

first appears in the Directory in 1894, with Mrs Catherine Howe as licensee. This stood on the opposite side of the road to the "Millbrook Hotel", and beyond the bridge over the creek[4]. It still stands there, but much altered in appearance from those early days.

The second hotel to appear in that year was at Jarrahdale Junction. It appears in the Directory variously as the "Serpentine Hotel" and the "Mundijong Hotel", in each case being shown as being at Jarrahdale Junction. The first recorded licensee was a Mr. Szeczinski, who appears to have held the licence from 1894 to 1900.[xlii]

Two More Locomotives[xliii]

It is significant that the volume of business was so great at this time that two more locomotives were purchased to handle the steadily increasing traffic. These were both bought in 1896 and were the "Jarrahdale" which was purchased from the railway contractors, Atkins and Law, and the "Rockingham", both locomotives being powerful "G" class engines built by Martins of Gawler, in South Australia. They each weighed 42 tons – very different from the little "Samsons" and the eight-ton "Governor Weld" of 1872.

Fremantle Inner Harbour Opened – 1897

In the following year, the great engineering enterprise of creating a secure harbour in the Swan River was at last completed, after five years of strenuous labour. When S.S. "Sultan" steamed in between the moles on May 4, 1897,

---

[4] There was no bridge over the Cooralong brook until around 1902. Previously there was only a ford. The first bridge consisted of three huge jarrah logs, decked over. The existing bridge was built about fifty years later.

Fremantle was at last able to offer a safe and convenient haven for ships, both sail and steam, of any size plying the outer oceans in those days. The effect of this on Jarrahdale, although still distant, was in the future to be very great, for now timber could be railed for shipment to Fremantle, while the new Government railway made it possible to also rail timber to Bunbury which was now becoming a major timber port. These two things reduced the importance of Rockingham which hitherto had been Jarrahdale's only export outlet. However, for some years yet, no advantage was taken of these new opportunities, and Rockingham continued to thrive.

9. *P2003.094 Head Office, "Rockingham Railway & Jarrah Forests Ltd." At Moore Street, East Perth, 1892*

10. 2003.004 Locomotive "Rockingham", at Jarrahdale c.1900

11. P2003.069 Rockingham Jetties, 1895

The Last Independent Jarrahdale Company

It was in 1897 that there was again a change in the ownership of the company, and once again it was probably (but not certainly) the need for extra capital which led to the business becoming the "Jarrahdale Jarrah Forests and Railways Ltd."

There does not appear to have been any marked changes in control of the company, and A. C. Munro certainly remained as Manager at Jarrahdale. Indeed, it looks as if it was really a matter of re-financing to meet the needs of the rapidly growing organisation. It is of great interest that soon after the re-organisation, the Deputy Chairman of the new company, James Martin, paid a visit to Jarrahdale, on behalf of the London Board of Directors and of the English shareholders. He arrived late in 1898 and left early in 1899. Being obviously impressed by what he had seen, Martin produced a report in 1899, after his return to England, calling it *"A short Description of a Visit to the Company's Mills and Forests"*. This little brochure is a veritable mine of information concerning the harbour at Rockingham and the Timber Station at Jarrahdale[xliv] then at its zenith of activity, with five mills in operation and yet another under construction.

Jarrahdale in 1899 – James Martin's Report

Extracts from this interesting and authoritative report are given below: -

Description of Concession. The Company's Concession is situated at Jarrahdale, in the Darling Mountains, Western Australia, about 35 miles south-west of Perth, the Capital, and is reached by the South-Western Railway to Jarrahdale Junction, 29 miles, and from thence by the Company's railway for six miles.

In shape the Concession is a square, 20 miles along each face, and comprises 250,000 acres or 400 square miles.

The country is very hilly, and heavily timbered, with usually a dense undergrowth. In the gullies no marketable jarrah timber is found, and only a scanty supply on granite hills but heavy timber on the ironstone ridges; fortunately, the principal part of the forest consists of ironstone.

In the gullies there is plenty of water, several rivers intersect the country, so there is no difficulty in obtaining an ample supply of water for the mills.

12. Jarrahdale township, in 1890s.

The Forest has been worked by the predecessors of the Company for fully 20 years, the result being that only one-fourth of the area has been, and is being, cut over, that is, out of an original area of 250,000 acres, 187,500 acres, or 300 square miles, are untouched, and even that portion cut over is still a dense forest, as no tree measuring less than six feet in circumference is taken. In those areas cut over at the outset, the smaller trees have grown to such an extent that much of it is now ready for falling. The Company has five mills at work, and the machinery for a sixth is now on the ground and in course of erection.

Harbour. The Company has a fine harbour at Rockingham, 23 miles from Jarrahdale, reached by the Company's own railway. The Harbour is formed by a bay, about 15 miles south of Fremantle, and is sheltered by Garden Island, which is about eight miles in length. The passage to the south of the island is shut in by a reef, forming a protection from south-west gales, whilst the opening to the north is known as the Challenger Passage.

Jetties. There are three jetties, one erected by the present Company and opened for traffic in October last. This jetty is 520 feet long and runs into 47 feet of water and can berth two large steamers or sailing ships. The centre jetty ... berth two large vessels" (while) "the third jetty can berth two small vessels. Six ships can therefore be berthed at one time.

The timber is brought in trucks by rail to the ships' sides, so that from the time the timber is felled, taken to the mills, and placed alongside the ships, it only passes over the Company's own railway, thus effecting great economy in cost as compared with any other timber mill in the Colony; as with one exception* the other timber companies have to pay railage over the Government lines, and also port and wharf dues.

Jarrahdale. The Jarrahdale Township is pleasantly situated six miles from Jarrahdale Junction and 600 feet above sea level. No. 1 mill, with the engineers', fitters', blacksmiths' and wheelwrights' shops, stores, and offices, are in the valley.

The Township is built on two slopes: a nice clear stream of water runs through the valley. There are three Churches – Wesleyan, Church of England, and Roman Catholic, the two-former having resident clergymen, the last visiting clergy. There is a State School, good Post and Telegraph Office and Savings Bank, Hotel, and small Public Hall and library and a large Hall with Stage, where entertainments are occasionally given. There is also a Police Station and Court House for the district, a Hospital and resident Doctor.

The whole property in the place, except for one house, either belongs to, or is under the control of, the Company.

Taking the whole of the Stations there are six State Schools, and a total population of about 1,200 souls, all depending upon Company's employment for their support.

In the valley at Jarrahdale the Company has a well-developed and well-watered orchard and kitchen garden, where fruits and vegetables are grown in profusion and sold to the workpeople.

Jarrahdale Junction. At Jarrahdale Junction the Company has a good siding with the Government Railway, and a crossing to the Harbour at Rockingham. They also have large sheds and offices and plenty of space for stacking and seasoning timber.

Mills James Martin then details all the six mills then operating or under construction on the Station. In particular, he notes that: -

No. 1 mill, at Jarrahdale, employed 32 men.

No. 2 mill also employed 32 men and was fed by logs hauled by eight teams of five horses each, or in all 40 horses.

No. 3 mill employed 20 men, fed by four teams or in all 20 horses.

No. 4 mill employed 22 men, four teams with 20 horses.

No. 5 mill at Jarrahglen, employed 20 men and four teams of horses.

No. 6 mill is in course of construction at Big Brook ... and is a fine Band-Saw mill.

"Besides the men engaged at the Mills, Offices, Shops, Stores and Harbour, the Company employs fallers and haulers, and possesses in all 140 fine, strong horses that would do credit to any establishment.

The men working at the several mills are a fine set of fellows and will stand comparison with those on any other similar property."

Perth Yard

"The Company also possesses an extensive Freehold Yard at Moore Street, Perth, near the Perth Railway Station; it adjoins the Government Railway and has a siding. There are two planing machines and a saw bench and extensive sheds and open spaces for storage, also good offices for the Staff, the Registered Offices of the Company being here."

Condition. "The Company owns four locomotives[5] (two large and two small) and the necessary proportion of trucks; these and the Mills and Railway are maintained in first-class order and condition.

The Company's Workshops are also in a very efficient condition; they turn out all castings and other work required for repairs to machinery, and manufacture and repair the huge jinker wheels etc., thus reflecting great credit upon Mr. Munro, the Manager, and his assistants."

Mr. Martin pays a tribute to Mr. A. C. Munro and says that ... "Mrs Munro is in a true sense his help-meet and does her best to look after the interests of the girls and women of the township. The girls were growing up in ignorance of the uses of the needle; she started a class which has an average attendance of about 30 girls. They meet every Saturday when plain and fancy needlework are taught and practised, and

---

[5] The two large locomotives were the "Jarrahdale" and the "Rockingham"; the two small ones were the "Pioneer" and the "Samson No. 1". "Samson No. 2" had been sold to the M.C. Davies Company of Karridale early in 1899. There was also the little shunter. "Governor Weld", which Martin does not mention.

while I was there the girls had a bazaar in aid of the Church funds and realised, in one day's sale, with that small population, nearly £40."

Mr. Martin then goes on to describe the Annual Sports ... "Hearing that drinking is a great failing at Timber Mill Stations, I determined to see for myself. I was present at the Annual Sports held every year on 26th December in the men's Recreation Ground at Jarrahdale. It is the great event of the year; a full programme was provided that took from ten till five to carry through. Nicely printed programmes were for sale, and a very enjoyable day ensued, the proceedings being enlivened by a band hired from Perth for the day. The competitions most enjoyed by the men were the 'hewing and sawing', competitors from each of the Company's mills entered, and the excitement among the comrades of the competitors was very great, much rivalry existing between the different mills ... the day was intensely hot, with a clear blue sky, and notwithstanding the heat, excitement and temptation to drink (as I noticed three booths erected by publicans, over which the Company at present has no control), and that the monthly pay-day was Christmas Eve, no case of open drunkenness, or roughness, or disturbance took place. The police in charge told me they had no trouble during the whole day ... The evening was wound up by a Ball held in the large Hall, the musicians occupying the stage, and I never saw a dance more heartily enjoyed by young and old. The floor was crowded, and it was at times difficult for the dancers to find room, but all went orderly and happily and was kept up from 8 pm to 4 am."

Mr. Martin concludes by saying ... "Briefly, the Shareholders possess a splendid, and to them inexhaustible forest, with six first-class mills, workshops, 60 miles of railway, four locomotives, the necessary complement of trucks, town yard, a fine harbour and three jetties."

The report is dated, "April 1899."

This then was the "Jarrahdale Timber Station", with its port of Rockingham, at the end of the nineteenth century. It had grown to greatness from small beginnings and had vastly changed from the early days of 1872. There was not, however, any great change in sawmilling methods, either at Jarrahdale or elsewhere in the industry. Modernisation was very slow in coming to the sawmills and a sawmiller of, say 1875, would have had no difficulty in recognising, or indeed using, a typical sawmill of 1900 – or even of 1950.

True, there were changes, important ones in their day, but they did not alter the early methods of handling and sawing timber.[xlv] For example, "live rollers" and "friction gear" was introduced, providing mechanical means for taking the heavy timber flitches up to, and through, the spinning saws, replacing the early method of hand winding gear. Eventually mechanical log-turners appeared a device installed at Jarrahdale's No. 5 mill early in the new century and long confined to that Station. At the output end of the mill, it was many decades before "sorting-tables" and "Green-chains" took over from the hand-propelled "galloping-out truck", but the basic method of the 1890's was still employed in the 1950's, and the saw-milling brought itself into line with other industries and introduced scientific automated equipment.

13. P2013.027 Log-hauling team and whim c1900

By the late 19th and early 20th century the mills at Jarrahdale were the best in the Colony but work in them was hard physical labour. The benchman pushed and strained, and walked many miles in the course of his working day, as he propelled his loaded bench-trolley up to and back from the saws; the "tailers-out" did the same on the other side of the saw; even men on the "dockers", where timber was cut to the required length, often had to pull, push and man-handle heavy pieces of timber all day long, a 54-hour working week being the rule for many years. Wages were low, the basic wage early in the present century was only 36/- per week and was only £4/10/- as late as 1940.

14. Mill Manager's house, Jarrahdale built for Neil McNeil, 1889. (Rail Heritage WA)

15. P2013.023 Workers houses at Jarrahdale 1924

For workers in the "bush" the hours of work were just as long and the wages almost as low as for the workers in the mill. Here in the bush the methods of falling and hauling logs changed but little for very many years. In the early days, and right up to the late 1940s the trees were felled with axe and saw, the fallers usually working in pairs. The work was laborious and hard, but somewhat better paid than was work in the sawmill, as the fallers were usually paid on a piece-work basis, the logs they cut being measured after arrival at the mill and the men paid based on the cubic contents of the logs they had felled.[xlvi]

16. P2003.266 A Bush Camp, early 1900s

Improved methods of log-hauling, the removal of the log from the stump where it was felled to the nearest log-landing on the bush railway line, where it was loaded onto a truck for transport to the sawmill, came somewhat earlier than did those for the actual falling.

Away back in the 1870s, teams of bullocks were employed to drag the logs, slung under the arches of the great high-wheeled jinkers, along the crude, roughly-cleared ("swamped") tracks. With each bullock team there was a teamster and one or more "swampers", whose task it was to clear the track ahead, as the bullocks slowly plodded their way to the mill or to the bush log-landing. Bullocks were strong, patient and willing, but they were very slow; from an early date, horses were used, normally in teams of eight, although at Jarrahdale in the "Nineties, five-horse teams were employed at some of the smaller mills. At times, when a particularly big log had to be dealt with teams, both of bullocks and/or horses had to be 'doubled-up' to drag the great weight along the rough track.

The huge vehicles, with their six or eight-foot wheels, known as "whims" and used for log hauling, were in almost universal use for well over sixty years. These "whims" were unknown in the very early days, a four-wheeled jinker being used instead. The jinker consisted of a rear axle, fitted with a heavy wooden logging arch. The front axle had a wooden turntable on it, which swivelled on an iron kingpin. The two axles had high wheels and were joined together with a pole, usually a redgum limb, with a natural bend at one end. Teamsters would search the bush far and wide to find limbs with suitable bends, which were rather like the 'knees" in the timbers of a ship. The whim is claimed by some experienced timber men to have been invented in Western Australia, at the old Canning mills, probably in the 1880s.[xlvii] The story is that a teamster, when bringing in a log, broke the pole of his jinker, and being a handy man, bound one end of the log to the broken end of the pole, and brought his log into the mill in triumph leaving the other wheels and the turntable in the bush. Finding that this rig did the job quite as well, or even better than the jinker, he made a practice of it, the idea being copied by others. Thus the 'whim" came into general use.

By the turn of the century there were far more horses than bullocks used for hauling logs, and as the years went by the bullocks gradually disappeared, although in some places they lingered on; there was a bullock team working at Nanga Brook, one of the Yarloop group of mills, as late as 1936.

The horses were kept in horse-lines near the bush camps, but at holiday times were brought into the mill town to "spell". Here at the mill township were large horse paddocks, and a great covered set of horse stalls, as well as an enormous forage shed, for the quantity of fodder these animals consumed was enormous. At the start of the Christmas holidays the great mob of horses coming into the town from the bush camps was one of the sights of Jarrahdale, and of many other big sawmilling centres. The grooms, and above all the veterinary officers were very important people indeed. The use of horses for log hauling continued at Jarrahdale right into the 1930s, and at other milling centres even longer.

The Mill Workers' Houses

For the most part, these houses were of a most unpretentious appearance, with the exterior walls of unpainted jarrah weatherboards, reddish in colour when new, but rapidly weathering into a uniform dull grey. The interior walls were lined with jarrah, which made the rooms very dark, unless the walls were painted, which they often were;[xlviii] usually, the tenants did this themselves, the company taking the view that, as no rent was paid until 1902, and even after then only 4/- or 5/- a week, it did not allow for unnecessary luxuries such as paint. The normal type of worker's house in the early 1900s cost the company £28 to erect, labour and materials. The roofs were of galvanised iron, as were the chimneys, which constituted a considerable fire hazard. The more fastidious occupants usually closed in one end of the back verandah to provide a bathroom, in which a galvanised iron bath was installed. The laundry, or "wash-house" was a weatherboard shed (unlined), built in the back garden, or yard. Water from the company's dam first pumped to large wooded overhead tans, was piped to all the houses, and connected to the kitchen and – if it existed – to the bathroom. Water for all purposes was heated on the kitchen stove, or in the wash-house copper, firewood for all household needs being supplied in dray loads by the company at a very low cost.

Many of the earlier houses were built by the employees themselves using timber "face-cuts", these being the first pieces sawn off a flitch of timber to provide a good "face" for the subsequent cut. These face-cuts were of irregular thickness and width but were supplied free to employees for house building. These do-it-yourself homes were very rough and crude to look at, but nevertheless very comfortable inside; indeed, many of the mill workers' cottages were far better furnished than those of their counterparts in the city.

No rent was charged for any of the employees' houses prior to 1902 when a very small charge was made, as mentioned above. A good number of these old cottages still exist and can still be seen at Jarrahdale, most of them being still occupied.

Quite the best house at Jarrahdale was that occupied for many years from 1893 onwards by successive managers of the Station. This house was built in the valley, beside the Corralong Brook, about a quarter of a mile up-stream from the original mill. It was built in the 1880s, for the then Managing Director of the "Neil McNeil Company", Neil McNeil himself,[xlix] who was a frequent visitor from the eastern colonies. He would come over from Melbourne by sea, then the only way to get to Western Australia, and disembark at Albany. Mill Managers also came by ship from Albany to Port Rockingham. From there, in the days before the Great Southern railway was built, he would take the mail coach to Perth, alighting at the 36 mile being met there by a horse and buggy, which then took him to Jarrahdale along the ten-mile bush track to Jarrahdale township. A permanent housekeeper was installed in the big house with its shady, wide verandahs. It was, in a way, the precursor of the Company's "Cottage", built for the use of visiting senior staff and important outside visitors, shortly after 1902. Soon after Munro became the mill manager in 1893 McNeil gave him this house as the "manager's House", which it has remained, being much as it was in the 1880s, and successive managers have occupied it. Prior to 1893, the then manager's house, a large and comfortable dwelling, stood a little further up the valley.[1] It has long since disappeared.

17. P2003.050 A Bush Landing c1905

18. P2003.076 A Log Landing, with A.C. Munro, Manager of Jarrahdale, 1899

19 P2003.174 The "Murray Arms" Hotel, Jarrahdale built c1886. The small building in the middle distance is the first office of the original Jarrahdale Road Board, 1913.

Bush Workers' Housing

Although the living conditions of the workers in the mill township were good, indeed very good by the standards of the time, those who worked in the bush – the fallers, teamsters, swampers and some of the railway maintenance crews – were by no means so well off, although the Company did all it could to make them comfortable. In the very early days, the "bush" was sufficiently close to the township to allow bush workers to live there, and travel to their work daily. However, as the closer trees were felled, their work became more and more distant, until it became necessary to create "bush camps" to accommodate them and thus avoid long journeys every morning and night.[h]

Bush Camps

These "bush camps" were semi-mobile, consisting of timber-framed huts with roof and walls of galvanised iron; sometimes the walls were of whitewashed hessian, being by no means waterproof. These huts were loaded on to railway trucks and taken out to the bush by locomotive. The site of the camp was always a major "bush log landing", a "log landing" being a place on the bush line where logs, after having been felled, barked, and trimmed, were dragged by teams, and dumped on the ground or on a rough platform or landing of logs to await transport to the sawmill.

When a rake of empty trucks arrived, the logs were pulled on to them by a wire rope, hauled by a steam winch which was permanently situated at the landing. The camp remained at the landing until the bush, i.e., the trees of millable size, had been cut out in the area, which could be a radius of a mile or a mile and a half, or even two miles from the landing. When this bush was cut out, the whole bush camp would be again loaded on to trucks and moved to a new log landing, several miles distant, and the whole process would begin anew.

In addition to the huts, these camps usually had a "bush boarding house" for single men, or such of the married workers who did not wish their wives and families to join them in the bush, and to suffer the discomforts of the rough living conditions: for they were rough, very rough indeed. In the summer the heat, dust and the flies were intolerable; the close presence of the horse lines made sure that there was no lack of flies. In winter, the mud surrounding the huts was often a foot deep, and the heavy rains of winter made the place a veritable "slough of despair". Even so, the courageous wives usually came with their menfolk and faced the deplorable conditions with determination and ingenuity to make sure that their men should have a home to come back to each night.[lii]

These bush camps were a feature of life at most of the big sawmilling stations – not only at Jarrahdale – and they endured for more than forty years, until the coming of the motor trucks made it once again possible for the workers to travel to and from bush to mill. The children of these devoted couples came too, and so large did the number of children become, that at a late stage – in the twenties – a mobile school, mounted on a railway truck chassis, was long in operation in the Jarrahdale bush. The mobile school operated only from October 1926 to March 1928, although as early as 1909 Peter O'Loughlan MLA wrote to the Minister for Education requesting a school on wheels.

Competition and Over-Production

One result of the opening of the South-West Government railway in 1893 was that it provided access to the forest past, or through which it made its way, and this quickly led to the erection of numerous sawmills along its route. Some of these, such as Waroona, Yarloop, Mornington, and Wellington, grew rapidly until they rivalled Jarrahdale in size and productive capacity. Although the vast increase in population in the 'Nineties had created a large demand, the new mills, competing with the old-established centres, such as Jarrahdale, soon brought about an over-production of sawn timber, creating a glut both in the local market and in those overseas.

The Jarrahdale company was better placed than most to face the savage competition of the late 'Nineties and, as we have seen, was at a peak of efficiency in 1899[liii] but even this well-established and well-managed concern felt the pressure of the times and early in the new century, of the six mills which were operating in 1899, all but two were soon forced to close. These two were No. 5, which boasted of that mechanical marvel, the "Symondson Log Turner", a great steel monster with hooked steel arms, which reached out, seized the log on its carriage and turned and manoeuvred it into the required position to be put through the huge saws of the "breaking-down" bench, where the first cuts were put into the log, to reduce it to smaller sizes, "flitches", which were then sent along rollers to the No. 1 and subsequent benches. The other mill was the nearly new No. 6, which also contained an unusual piece of equipment at its breaking-down bench. This was a "gunshot" log carriage, which needed much skill and experience to operate. One day this carriage lived up to its name by shooting a huge flitch right through the twin saws, wrecking the rig completely.[liv] Fortunately, no one was hurt. There was a similar carriage at the Canning Mill, but it appears they had so many problems that they were not installed at any other mills.

The New Century

On 1 January 1901 the Colony of Western Australia ceased to exist, and the State of Western Australia came into being as a part of a wider Commonwealth, amid rejoicings which were marred later in the month by the news of the death of the great Queen Victoria. According to police and newspaper reports, at least ten fatalities occurred before 1901. Records show the first railway death in 1879. Jarrahdale had a private sorrow, for it was on 20th April 1901 that the Jarrahdale-Rockingham railway suffered another fatal accident.[iv] On that afternoon both the locomotives "Pioneer" and "Samson No. 1" were at No. 6 mill, each with a train load of sawn timber and hewn sleepers to be taken to Jarrahdale. Both left at about the same time, with "Pioneer" leading and "Samson" following behind. Shortly after leaving, a very steep hill was encountered, and it was the practice of the engine crew of the second train to wait on a flat stretch of track for the leading train to surmount the grade and proceed on its way. Once the leading locomotive, in this case the "Pioneer", was over the hill, it would be the turn of the second train, pulled by the "Samson" to tackle the hill ... In this instance, the driver of the "Samson" stopped on the flat as was the practice, and while he waited proceeded to oil around his engine, and was lying down on the running plate, oiling underneath, when the fireman heard a terrific rumble coming down the hill and looking up saw the trucks formerly in charge of the "Pioneer", bearing down on him out of control. He shouted to the driver Charles Daws to jump clear but Daws being hard of hearing did not hear him especially as his engine was blowing-off steam. In the ensuing crash the driver was fatally injured. The manager, A. C. Munroe, immediately organised a special train to take Daws to hospital in Perth, but unfortunately, he was dead on arrival. The body was brought back to Jarrahdale and given an impressive funeral in the Jarrahdale cemetery where his grave is still to be seen.

20. P2021.016 The Railway disaster of April 1901 (Loc. Samson)

This unhappy event cast a gloom over the whole Station, but apart from this the year was a good one despite the severe competition that the company was facing.

Shipping was quite brisk at Rockingham no less than twenty-seven vessels arriving during the year, eight of them stammers, the biggest number that the port had handled for years. Much of the timber exported consisted of paving blocks which by this time had become very popular for street paving both in Australia and in England. It is paradox that although it would seem that these little "wood bricks" would be economical to produce and would provide greater utilisation of short lengths of timber, this was not quite the case, as at this time the buyers demanded a 9in. x 3in. section which meant that the timber was first cut into 9in. x 3in. longer lengths (usually 4ft. to 14ft.) and subsequently docked into 4½in. block lengths, much timber which would not give the desired 9in. width being wasted. Later, 6,7 and 8in. sections were accepted with a consequent economy of timber. While these blocks were awaiting shipment at Rockingham, they were stacked in a huge wooden box a hundred feet long and covered with sawdust to preserve them from the hot sun.[lvi]

The Cattleduffers[lvii]

Another, highly illegal, activity which flourished at that time, as it had done for some years in the '90s, was at "Hall's Station Gully", not far from Jarrahdale township, where stolen cattle were slaughtered and the carcasses despatched to a ring of metropolitan butchers, who were "in the game". As this was naturally a very secret business and never came officially to light, no details of it exists, but the fact was well known to Jarrahdale residents at the time.

Although the Jarrahdale company was doing reasonably well, the competition in the industry was forcing prices down to a disastrous level. By 1900 it was clear that the situation must be taken in hand and the chaotic, cutthroat situation stabilised. This work was taken in hand by Henry Teesdale Smith, the capable and energetic General Manager of the C.& E. Millar Company, which had first started milling timber at

Torbay, near Albany, in 1884, mainly to supply sleepers and other railway timbers for the Great Southern Railway, which the Millars' Company was just starting to build.

In 1896-97 the Millars' organisation floated a company in England calling it "Millars' Karri and Jarrah Company Limited", which rapidly expanded its sawmilling activities in the forests opened by the new South-West railway. This company, having access to considerable finance in London, was in a strong position to bring about a massive re-organisation of the whole timber industry in Western Australia.

The Great Amalgamation[lviii]

After two years of hard work the re-organisation was completed, when eight of the major sawmilling companies amalgamated to form in 1902 one great organisation under the name of the leading company "Millars' Karri and Jarrah Company Limited", which rapidly brought order out of chaos and put the industry on a secure and profitable footing.

The four leading companies in this new and powerful "combine" were Millars themselves, the Canning Jarrah Timber Co., the M. C. Davies Karri and Jarrah Co. and, most notable of all, the "Jarrahdale Jarrah Forests and Railways Co. Ltd".

The Chairman of the local board of Directors was E. H. Wittenoom, other members including Edwin Millar, William McMurtrie, and A. J. McNeil. Teesdale Smith was the Managing Director. The new company had mills at Canning, Jarrahdale, Waroona, Waterous, Yarloop, Mornington, Wellington, Worsley, Newlands, Jarrahwood, Karridale, Boranup, Jarrahdene and Denmark, and these produced about 75% of all the timber sawn in the State.

From 1902 onwards the famous pioneering Jarrahdale enterprise lost its identity and became one of the many companies which, under the banner of "Millars", were now as a combination, controlling the timber industry of the State, and as with Jarrahdale, Rockingham lost its pre-eminence although for a moment it seemed that the amalgamation would give Rockingham a new and even greater importance.

This was due to the proposal by Teesdale Smith, that Rockingham should become again the principal timber port, by linking up the "combine's" sawmills which ran in a chain from Wellington and Mornington in the south to Jarrahdale and the Canning mills in the north, by connecting the bush lines of each mill to the Jarrahdale-Rockingham line. This would have meant that by far the greater part of the timber cut for export at all the "combine's" mills would have been shipped through Rockingham making that port a very important place indeed.

Having this idea in mind it was apparent to the board of Directors that as ships were now getting much larger, it would be necessary to improve the access to the Rockingham jetties by cutting a channel through the Parmelia sandbank over which the water was so shallow that only small vessels could cross it. The other entrance to Cockburn Sound, the Challenger passage, was even more difficult to deepen owing to its rocky nature.

Accordingly, the Chairman of Directors of the company Sir Edward Wittenoom wrote to the Fremantle Harbour Trust on 3rd February 1903 requesting that the removal "of a sufficient portion of the Parmelia Bank to enable ships drawing say 20 feet of water going in and out of Rockingham. Owing to the shallowness of the entrance to this port this company finds it necessary to arrange for most of their timber being shipped from Bunbury."

However, the Harbour Trust was not favourable to the idea, and replied to that effect on 11th February 1903, saying that "such an approach would be impracticable and dangerous in a gale from the West."

Shortly afterwards the State Government not surprisingly turned down Teesdale Smith's proposal to link up the combines railway lines as this would have short-circuited the almost new South-West Government line from Bunbury to Perth, over which much timber freight was being profitably carried.

After these two rebuffs the grand scheme was therefore dropped, the result being that in the future Jarrahdale timber for export would be railed to Bunbury while for Rockingham it was the beginning of the end. So, the Board made its hard decision; Rockingham port was to be allowed to fade away and die. This was by no means obvious to Jarrahdale and Rockingham residents in 1903; indeed, the year was a busy one at the port, for 17 vessels came in that year, and at the same time two large lighters were built on the beach at Rockingham destined to carry Jarrahdale timber to Bunbury to supplement that sent by rail. However, next year in 1904 it was obvious that a drastic change was close at hand as only five vessels used the port and in the following year only four. This number decreased to three in 1906 to one only in 1907 while the very last ship to come to Rockingham was the little S.S. "Una" in 1908.

Jarrahdale as Part of the "Combine"

Although Rockingham was fading into obscurity Jarrahdale was full of life and prospered exceedingly in the early years of the new century. After the amalgamation of 1902 Jarrahdale was one of the finest assets of the great new company – "Millars' Karri and Jarrah Co. Ltd." From that time onward Jarrahdale, with its associated depot at Jarrahdale Junction now Mundijong concentrated on the trade with Perth while timber for export now shipped mainly from Bunbury became a secondary consideration thus reversing the position which had obtained for so many years. For Jarrahdale, expansion was very much the order of the day.

In the decade which followed the amalgamation of 1902 timber became the "glamour industry" of Western Australia. Some of the lustre had faded from gold mining. Gold exports declined in value after 1903 (by 50% by 1914) while timber steadily increased to twice its former value. In those years, timber held much the same popular interest and esteem as did minerals, iron ore and nickel in the 1960s and '70s; public interest was great as timber production soared, and in this increase, Jarrahdale played a full part.

Increased Production and a New "Board Mill"

Very soon after the amalgamation, Teesdale Smith came to Jarrahdale and his first words to Munro (who had remained as manager) were: – "I want more timber Munro and more boards." Munro replied, "If you want more timber and more boards you will have to enlarge our mills and it is not payable cutting boards in large mills." Having discussed the situation, it was decided to enlarge No. 5 and No. 6 mills to enable them to cut 80 loads per day between them and at the same time to erect another mill specially to cut boards. This was situated about halfway between Jarrahdale and Nos. 5 and 6 mills which both supplied the new board mill with flitches of timber.[lix]

Notable Foremen at Jarrahdale

The mill foremen at Jarrahdale and indeed at all the great sawmilling centres of the timber industry were key men who carried a great responsibility as it was upon their experience and efficiency that the success of the mill depended; their technical skill complemented the overall administrative work of the mill manager. Two of the most famous of these foremen were Joe Lewis and Charles Baskerville who between them had fifty-six years as foremen at Jarrahdale.

Joe Lewis became mill foreman in the year 1883 when only 19 years old. Like his mill manager Munro Lewis rose to responsibility at an early age and played a great part in the success of Jarrahdale mill. He had a numerous family and was always liked for his kindly attitude to employees, often finding them work of some kind when they were unemployed. He was mill foreman until 1926 thus serving in that capacity for nearly 44 years. He died in 1928 being long remembered at Jarrahdale not only for his ability but also for his fine qualities as a man.

21. P2015.004 Mobile Bush School, Jarrahdale 1920s

Charles Baskerville was born at Busselton in 1881. His father worked at the old Ballarat company's mill at Wonnerup. When still a child Charlie's family moved to Bunbury travelling on a bullock wagon, as this was long before the days of the railway, and even the roads were little more than mere tracks. He went to school in Bunbury and then, in 1889, the family moved to Karridale, going by sea in S.S. *"Bullara"* to Hamelin, then a busy port for timber shipments from the M. C. Davies company's mills. Young Charles left school in 1894 and got his first job in the Karridale mill painting timber etc. and earning 2/6 per week. He rapidly gained experience in the mill, benching etc. and then transferred to Boranup on the big bench and thence to Jarrahdene mill four miles further on and later still to Jarrahwood which he reached by coach to Busselton, then by Government train to Wonnerup and by Company train (Jarrahwood Paving Co.) to Jarrahwood. From Jarrahwood he went to Newlands where he saw the excitement of a gold strike at Donnybrook which unfortunately came to nothing. In the early 1900s, it was not always easy to find a job and until 1907 he worked at many mills including the 11 Mile Mill of the Gill McDowell Company at Waroona and at Hoffman's, one of the Yarloop group of mills, Karridale once again then back to Waroona and to William's Mill at Cookernup. From there he went to Wellington Mills in 1907 as rip benchman and was later appointed foreman of that mill, holding that position until 1918, when he became the foreman of a new board mill at Mundijong, this being part of the Jarrahdale timber station, remaining there until that mill was closed in 1929 at the onset of the great trade depression, when he was transferred to Jarrahdale as foreman of the "No. 2" mill. When that mill also closed in December 1930 he was sent to Treesville, one of the

Mornington group of mills, and when this mill also closed in 1931, he returned to Mundijong, going back to re-open Treesville in 1935, when the depression was starting to lift. However, he was not there long, being again transferred, this time, back to Jarrahdale where he was the foreman on the "No 2" mill when it reopened in 1935. He held this position for nineteen years – until 1954. Afterwards, being then 73 years of age, he remained as a saw-filer until he retired in 1961 at the age of 80.

It is pleasing to note that today he is living in honoured retirement at the age of 90. His career is a good example of the wide experience gained by many of the notable mill foremen who made their mark in the timber industry of Western Australia.

Of equal importance to the Mill Foremen were the Bush Foremen, who had the exacting task of controlling the log falling and hauling in the forest. Notable bush foremen of the period, and right into the Twenties, were Bill Coglan and Bob Rutherford, the latter becoming for many years the manager of Nanga Brook, one of the sawmills of the Yarloop group.

There were many remarkable "characters" on the sawmills of that period, ranging from the astute and crafty "Kelly the Mug", manager of East Kirup, of whom many tales, not always complimentary, are told, down to such lesser figures as "Jack the Ripper", also of Kirup, white-bearded "Straight-up" Smith of Mornington and "Santo" of Jarrahdale, who was believed to have worked as a lad on a Spanish pirate ship before he settled down at Jarrahdale. "Santo" worked at No. 6 mill, and he and his mate, Hughes, each lived in huts on the present road from Jarrahdale to the modern Serpentine Dam. Unfortunately, although these colourful figures are well remembered, in most cases the story of their early lives is nowhere recorded.

Soon a very large stacking yard developed around the new board mill, where vast quantities of boards were stripped-out for drying. Both Teesdale Smith and Munro were very proud of the enlarged mills and of the great stock of boards which had been created, so much so, that they had several photographs taken of them and of the stacking yard, copies of these pictures, all dated 1905 being displayed with pride in the company's "Cottage", where they remained for over fifty years, as a reminder of the "combines" early days at Jarrahdale.

The Company's "Cottage"

In those days Jarrahdale was very much one of Millars' show places and numerous important people came to visit and inspect it. To accommodate these visitors Teesdale Smith had a large and commodious building erected in about 1902-3. This was on the right-hand side of the road, just as it entered the township. The Post Office was almost opposite and beyond the Post Office beside the creek was the site of the original mill of 1872. This "Cottage" was surrounded by magnificent oak trees some of which are still standing, and in its time saw many scores of important visitors come and go. A housekeeper was installed who always kept a very good table, and a good store of wines and spirits was always on hand. Apart from business visitors and members of the Company's senior staff, Munro, who was an enthusiastic Mason, frequently entertained parties from Perth lodges at the "Cottage", an opportunity which was greatly appreciated by those concerned. It is sad to relate that this locally famous old building was pulled down in 1962, after some sixty years of useful life.

22. Henry Teesdale Smith, General Manager of Millars' Karri & Jarrah Co. Ltd. 1907

"Cope's Boarding House"[lx]

For many years before the "Cottage" was erected, a boarding house – mainly for mill employees – had stood on the same site. This boarding house was presided over for a very long time by Mrs. Ellen Cope, who was one of the institutions of Jarrahdale.

Mrs. Cope who was born in County Cork, in Ireland, in 1846 came to Jarrahdale in the 1880s, where her husband, James Cope, worked in the mill. Mrs. Cope was a very capable woman of decided views, which she never feared to express. It is said that she presided at the head of the long dining table and ruled her boarders with firmness.

Many years before the amalgamation, the boarding house was destroyed in an unusual way. For some time, Mrs. Cope had been apprehensive of danger from a large Jarrah tree that grew next to the building, almost over-shadowing it. She therefore decided to have it removed and sent for Jarrahdale's best faller to look at it and see if he could fell it without damaging the building. When he arrived, Mrs. Cope said ... "Well, George (we will call him George) ... can you do the job?"; after studying the situation, "George" said with confidence ... "Yes, I can do it; leave it to me," and went off to get his mate and his tools. "George", an expert faller, proceeded to scarp the tree with his axe, taking the greatest care that it was just in the right place, and then with his mate proceeded to cut the back with his cross-cut saw. Soon the tree began to creak and groan; the fallers stood back, and the tree began to fall, slewing as it fell, to come down with a mighty crash – right on top of the building, wrecking it completely! It is said that the scorn which Mrs. Cope poured on the unfortunate "George" was a classic piece of vituperation, being long remembered by all who heard it.

The boarding house was an important place – many men depended on it for board and lodging, so Mrs. Cope was given the old Hall, next to the post office, which was fitted out as a new boarding house without delay. This building, which was noteworthy for having its ceilings and walls formed of stamped metal, is no longer there.

Long after this disaster, Mrs. Cope had to contend with another problem. When the new (Millars') Company took over in 1902, the management decided that all employees would have to pay a small rent, as was the case on all their other mills. The rent was small, and the men, after some grumbling, accepted this impost without much demur; Mrs. Cope, however, was not going to put up with that sort of thing, claiming that the building was hers by right of long occupancy. She was so determined about this that she engaged a well-known Perth solicitor, one "Dickey" Haynes, to fight the case for her. She won it, but the proviso that she did, indeed, own the land on which the building stood, but *not an inch outside the walls*! Mrs. Cope's remarks in this case would also have been worth hearing; unfortunately, they were not recorded. Mrs Cope died in 1917, her husband having died in 1900. The couple had five children, two boys, William James, and Thomas John and three daughters, Ellen, Elizabeth and Mary, and many descendants are still living in Western Australia.

Early in the century the charge made to boarders was 15/- a week; later, as wages rose, it became £1, and then 25/-.

23. Joe Lewis, Mill Foreman 1883-1926 with sons c1914

24. P2015.006 "Cope's Boarding House", early 1900's

25. P2018.155 Mrs Cope and her daughter Nellie Cope early 1900s

26. Group outside Cope's Boarding House, 1898.
James Cope (1824 to 1900) first on right in front row.

The Great Strike of 1907[lxi]

For some years there had been discontent amongst timber workers generally over the low wages paid, but there was no timber workers' union to take the matter up until 1902. In the following year there was much talk of a strike, but this was averted. The trouble came to a head again in 1906, due to a new award which had reduced wages by 6d. per day, and the union decided to strike in protest. The strike was widespread throughout the industry. It started in March 1907 and lasted fourteen weeks. Practically every milling centre was affected, including especially those of the "combine". As the demand for timber was urgent, Millars' K. & J. Co. Ltd. decided to try to keep at least one mill working to meet the most urgent orders. They selected No. 5 mill at Jarrahdale for the purpose – they could not use No. 6 as they had no one capable of working the "Gunshot" log carriage, the regular benchman being among the strikers.

To man the mill, the Company transferred many staff from other mills to Jarrahdale; "Staff" were not members of the union, but were foremen, office workers and the like. This scratch crew was able to keep the mill going, after a fashion, for the duration of the strike, while the regular Jarrahdale crew watched their amateur efforts with amusement, yet without rancour. Help and financial aid poured into the union funds from all over Australia, the sympathies of the public being obviously on the side of the strikers.

Week followed week; month followed month with no end in sight. Meanwhile, urgent orders for timber were piling up and the London Directors of the Company were getting more and more worried. At one stage there was a suggestion that the union be given one mill to work in co-operation with the Company, but this idea fell through. June came, and at last both sides were desperate for a solution, realising that the struggle could not go on much longer.

It is related that one day the General Manager of the Company, Teesdale Smith, and the Manager of Jarrahdale, A. C. Munro, were at Jarrahdale, standing on the verandah of the main office, discussing the gloomy situation, when a clerk from the post office arrived with a telegram. This was a cable from the London Board of Directors saying, "Strike gone on too long; agree to men's terms." As Teesdale Smith and Munro were reading and discussing this message, a small group of workers were seen to be coming along the road towards the office. When they arrived, they proved to be representatives of the union, and their leader said: "We have had enough; we agree to your terms!" Teesdale Smith put the telegram in his pocket and replied he was glad that the men had come to their senses at last, and that a resumption of work would be arranged immediately.[6]

The strike, which had started in March, ended on 25th June, relief at the ending of the struggle being universal. Celebrations were held at Jarrahdale on 5th, 6th and 7th July, the Company granting full pay to the workers during these days. A Ball, a big picnic with a cruise around Garden Island – although it was mid-winter – were held to mark the occasion, and these holidays over, the mills at Jarrahdale resumed their normal activities. This was the first and only widespread strike experienced by the industry from its earliest days up to the present time.

Changes in Local Management

Shortly after the end of the strike Teesdale Smith resigned as General Manager, to take up contracting again in the Eastern States. He was succeeded by A. J. McNeil, the brother of Neil McNeil, while A. C. Munro left Jarrahdale to become the Superintendent of all the Company's mills, remaining in that capacity until 1938, when he retired at the ripe age of 80.

At Jarrahdale, F. L. ("Tim") Brady took over the management, he and Munro having a friendly argument as to who became Superintendent and who the Manager of Jarrahdale. Brady remained as Manager until 1935.

At this period the Head Office of the Company was at Lord Street, Perth, where the combined offices of Millars' and the former head offices of both the Canning and the Jarrahdale companies, with their associated timber yards and joinery works, made an imposing industrial complex. Shortly afterwards[lxii] the former premises of Coombe Woods and Co. were taken over to add to the group. This Lord St., Moore St.,

---

[6] Communicated by the late Maj. R. A. Geedes, who stated that he was present at the time.

Coombe Woods complex remained for well over fifty years the heart of the "Combine's" local trading business.

It was also at this time that the main board-seasoning yard was transferred to Jarrahdale Junction, now known as Mundijong, where a large timber dressing mill was established.

The Coming of the Steam Log-Haulers

In the years following the great strike, the mills at Jarrahdale became busier than ever; the demand seemed to be insatiable, and thought was given to improving the methods of log-hauling (as described above) and putting it on a more modern and efficient basis, "Steam Haulers" being introduced during the years 1910-12. These were powerful steam winches mounted on a locomotive chassis, on which a boiler was also set up. These "Log-Haulers" were taken out to the bush by the railway and securely anchored on a spur line close to a bush log landing. A heavy steel rope, coiled on an enormous drum, also mounted on the chassis, was dragged out into the bush by horses to where the fallers were working, often a distance of well over a mile.

At intervals, the wire rope was led through a heavy steel block, fastened to the butt of a tree, the end of the rope being attached to the log which had to be brought in. "Whistle boys" were stationed along the line of pull, to signal when to pull and when to stop, for the Hauler was well out of sight of the log it was pulling for most of the way. When the signal was given, the great steam winch began to pull, and as Hammond had remarked in his description of the "Thomason Steamer" in 1872 ... " ... the log had to come when that engine was pulling." It was an impressive sight to see a huge fifty- or sixty-foot log plunging its way through the forest, attached by a wire rope to a far distant winch. "Swampers" were employed to clear the track it was making as it forced its way along.

These "Haulers" were expensive to build and to maintain, being nearly as costly as a locomotive, and for that reason were not widely employed; only the big companies at their most important mills could afford to use them. They remained in use until the early "Thirties, when the next important change occurred – the coming of the tractor.

Two New Mills

To increase output still further and to keep itself in the forefront of sawmilling technique, the Company built two new large mills in 1912-13. These were built back in Jarrahdale itself, near the site of, but further up-stream than the original No. 1 mill. These new mills were built end to end, No. 1 having an output of 50 loads per day, and No. 2 an output of around 25 loads. Both No. 5 and No. 6 mills were then closed, the famous "Symondson Log Turner" being installed in the new No. 1, which became a most famous mill, being probably the largest mill in Australia. It had 28 benches and was two-sided, with benches working right and left of the breaking-down saws, which, with the spectacular "Symondson Turner" made it an imposing sight. Hosts of people went to Jarrahdale to see it at work, including in later years, the members of the Inter-State Forestry Conference who came in 1917, and two years later, in 1919, the famous French General Pau, who led a trade mission to Australia in that year.

St. George's House[lxiii]

It was in this time of high prosperity that "Millars' Karri and Jarrah Co. Ltd." was re-organised, to become "Millars Timber and Trading Co. (1912) Limited", a name which held an honoured place in the history of Western Australia for nearly sixty years. A new Head Office was also built at a cost of £60,000 in St. George's Terrace, the principal area of Trade and Finance in the city of Perth. The magnificent new building, one of the stateliest in the "Terrace", remained the Head Office of the Company until 1971, when a further, and major re-organisation took place. Prior to these, the company's head offices had been successively in Princes Buildings, Perth, and then Lord St., as mentioned above.

These were the days when the West Australian hardwood industry reached a peak of production never again to be attained. In 1912, Millars' mills alone produced 97,000,000 super feet of timber (over 161,000 loads) the next highest year being in 1926 when 62,000,000 super feet (102,000 loads) were turned out. Exports flourished, and Bunbury, now the main timber shipping port, was a forest of masts and yards as sailing ships and many steamers were in the port all through the year. It was in 1913 that Millars finally abandoned their former port of Rockingham, while Jarrahdale flourished exceedingly.

Although the port was closed, trains continued to run from Jarrahdale to Rockingham for more than thirty years, although infrequently. Under the terms of the original agreement, a train had to run over the line at least once every year, and this was done to take a supply of firewood to replenish stocks at the Rockingham firewood depot and to supply the requirements of the Port Hotel. In addition, a regular "Picnic Train" ran every summer, taking Jarrahdale residents for a day at the seaside. There is good evidence to suggest that the picnic train ran for many more years, possibly seventy years. These runs were always popular, and in the

"Twenties were often quite big affairs, run in co-operation with the West Australian Government Railways. The most famous occasion was in 1924, when special trains were run from Perth, from Dwellingup and Pinjarra to Mundijong, to link up with the Jarrahdale train at Mundijong. The last of these "Excursion" trains ran in 1943, ending a custom which had then lasted for seventy years.

The World War

All this great activity was slowed, almost to a halt, with the outbreak of War in August 1914. Many mills closed, not to re-open until the war was over, but some had to keep going, and fortunately Jarrahdale was one of these, as although exports had vastly declined, timber was still needed for use within the State, where building, although much reduced, continued at a lower level, and the timber trains to Mundijong continued to be a common sight, though less frequently than before. Although Jarrahdale did not close, many of her workers enlisted in the Services and "did their bit' in the common cause. Indeed, Jarrahdale contributed more than her fair share of men to the Army, and of these the War Memorial at Jarrahdale testifies that no less than 41 made the supreme sacrifice, the names listed being almost a roll call of the principal families of the town and district. It was during these war years that Jarrahdale was host to the Forestry Conference, as mentioned above.

Post-War Jarrahdale

With the coming of peace in November 1918 and the gradual return home of the troops from overseas, the mills began to open once more, while shipping slowly returned to its normal peace-time activities. We have already noted the visit in 1919 of the French Trade Mission, headed by General Pau. The members of the delegation and especially its leader was received with great enthusiasm by the people of Jarrahdale.

Jarrahdale quickly returned to its former intense activity, as train-load after train-load of jarrah rolled down the rails to Mundijong, where the timber stacks in the depot grew larger and larger, until by the end of the "Twenties there were over 15,000 loads of boards in strips, besides a vast quantity of other timbers. In these years, only one other of Millars' depots exceeded Mundijong in size; this was Yarloop, where at the same period, over 30,000 loads were held in stock.

27. P2015.014 The Big Strike. 8 Hours. Millars

28. *St George's House 1913*

29. *P2003.56 Jarrahdale-Rockingham excursion train, 1924.*

The demand for railway sleepers in these years was tremendous, cargo after cargo being shipped through Bunbury, mainly to South Africa. Paving blocks and longer length paving (Usually 8 or 9 x 3) were produced in great quantities, while the call for building timber in Perth grew louder than ever, and the demand was great.

In these years the activity at Jarrahdale was intense, as train loads went down to Mundijong, some destined for waiting ships at Bunbury where, in the "Twenties, the South African Railways ran a shuttle service of steamers, the *"Huntress"*, *"Apolda"*, the *"Seattle"*, and others to and from Cape Town and Durban with full cargoes of sleepers and crossings, while much more timber went to the metropolitan market in Perth, or to replenish stocks at the ever-growing Mundijong yard. During the last year of the war, in 1918, a new board mill was built at Mundijong, where the depot, despite war-time problems, had difficulty in meeting the demand for dressed flooring and mouldings.

In April 1920 there was another fatal accident on the railway, when Tommy Cope, a guard on a log rake was killed. He was walking along the line of moving log trucks when he slipped and fell, being run over, and killed immediately. The accident was not noticed at the moment it happened, but when shortly afterwards he was missed, a search revealed his body near the points just outside the Jarrahdale mill.

The work of a guard on the log rakes was always full of danger. Quite often a guard would walk or run along the top of the logs when the train was moving, usually for the purpose of taking up or letting down the brakes, and in winter especially when the logs were wet and slippery it was a very dangerous practice. There were several similar accidents at other sawmills from time to time.

An Unlucky Fire

It was unfortunate that just as trade was recovering from the effects of the war, that the "No 2" mill (which had been built in 1901) was destroyed by fire on 6th May 1920.

A vivid impression of this disaster is recalled by Stan Hearne, who at the time was employed as a junior loco cleaner. He had only just entered the service of the company, starting his duties on 4th May, just two days before the mill was burnt. He recalls that on the night of 5th/6th he was on shift work in the locomotive shed, and was having an unauthorised doze when, very early in the morning, his mate suddenly seized him by the leg and shook him awake. Stumbling out of the shed, rubbing the guilty sleep out of his eyes, he saw an amazing and never-to-be-forgotten sight. The sawmill was one vast sheet of flame – ablaze from end to end. The spectacle was awe-inspiring, as the flames roared through the mill, while every now and then the roof timbers fell with a shower of sparks. There was nothing he could do about it; there was nothing anybody could do about it when one of the old-time sawmills was well alight. All he could do was watch, with all the many Jarrahdale residents who were awakened by the fire, while the flames roared to a conclusion, and the mill was destroyed.

Norman Temperley Becomes General Manager

In the following year, 1921, A. J. McNeil retired from the position of General Manager of the Company, which he had held since 1907, his place being taken by Norman Temperley. Temperley had come out from the London Office of the Company in 1908, to take over as Secretary from the previous occupant of that position, Thomas Garvin. He remained as General Manager until his retirement in 1956, being a frequent visitor to Jarrahdale over a period of forty years.

The Great Depression of the "Thirties

The busy period of prosperity continued right through the

'Twenties, until the shadow of the world-wide trade depression fell across the scene. Starting with the collapse of the Wall Street stock market in October 1929, the Great Slump spread over the entire world, reaching Jarrahdale by the end of the year. It then became apparent that in relation to the shrunken demand, the timber industry was heavily over-stocked, and a drastic reduction in production was needed. Sawmill after sawmill closed and thousands of mill workers became unemployed, most of them being forced on to "unemployment relief" – the "dole" of 7/- per week for single men and 14/- per week for married men, and a dreadful situation arose with appalling speed.

At Jarrahdale the first effect of the slump was that the big No. 1 mill closed in December 1929, being followed a year later, in December 1930, by the closure of No. 2 mill.[lxiv] The blow was made even more dreadful by the belief that these mills would never open again, it being thought by the Company at the time that, when trade improved, the big mills would be replaced by smaller "spot mills", built in the bush at some distance from the township. So, on Christmas Eve 1930, the saws ceased to whine through the jarrah logs at Jarrahdale, and a dreadful silence settled over the valley, where for sixty years the sound had never ceased for long.

In this year, too, the Millbrook Hotel closed, never to be re-opened. The Millbrook opened in 1891 and closed in 1930 at the height of The Great Depression. It re opened in 1935 and finally closed in 1938.

One factor which undoubtedly influenced the closure of the mills was the fact that on 31st December 1929 the 40-year term of the famous "Jarrahdale Concession" came to an end, so that from that time onwards the Company had to face the payment of timber royalties, which it had so far escaped at

Jarrahdale, this meaning further increased costs at a time when trade was at its lowest ebb. At this time the working and conservation of the forests had been for ten years under the control of the Forests Department, which had been established by the Forests Act of January 1919, with the task of the classification of timberlands and the eventual dedication of State Forests. The easy-going methods of the early sawmillers, who cut trees where and when they wanted, were replaced by a system of "Sawmilling Permits", all under the supervision of the new Department. By 1920 all payments to the Crown for logs sawn at the mills were on a royalty basis. For this measure which undoubtedly was one of the best devised for the benefit of the industry and of the State, the names of C. E. Lane-Poole, the first Conservator, and of S. L. Kessell, who replaced Lane-Poole in 1926, will be long remembered with honour throughout the industry.

A Forestry office was first established at Jarrahdale in the 'Twenties, and a few years later a District office was established at Gleneagle, on the Albany Road, about ten miles from Jarrahdale, where a large settlement grew up to which, in 1938, the former mobile "Bush School" was transferred from Jarrahdale, where it had stood unused and derelict for a number of years. One of the first and most notable of the professional Forests Department officers was Mr. A. C. Harris, who later was Conservator of Forests from 1953 to 1969. In the late 'Sixties a District Office was set up at Jarrahdale itself, which is now of substantial size, under the control of Forester Frank Quicke.

The years which followed the closure of the mills were hard; indeed, the mills were silent, the skilled workers dispersed, many of them going to the terrible 'labour camps', where they dragged out an existence in huts or under canvas, doing such part-time work as the State Government – itself desperate and under great pressure – could find them. The largest of these camps was in the Harvey district, at Myalup and Stonehouse, near the "Old Coast Road', then a mere track, where unemployed men from every trade and every area were assembled – places of poverty, despair, and broken hopes. Other workers spread throughout the State, while their money lasted, looking for work which rarely came. The "Basic Wage", for those few who were fortunate enough to get jobs, went down to £3/9/- a week; these were bad years, worse than the war-time years by far. 1932 was the worst year of all; the slump hit rock-bottom and there was scarcely a mill in the whole State still working and the future was bleak indeed.

However, Jarrahdale was never deserted. There was always a little work offering, for the few. Most of the activity, such as it was, was at Mundijong, where some boards were still being converted into dressed flooring and some scantling still being despatched from existing stocks to keep up a supply to the metropolitan yards.

30. Alfred Cook, Manager of Jarrahdale 1935-1958

31. P2005.112 The New Sawmill of 1968

A rail car had been built, and this ran up and down from Jarrahdale as required. It could haul a large railway truck – an "R" or an "RA" – up the hill and was more economical to run than a locomotive. Gradually the drab and dreadful years passed and at last the depression began to lift. The vast accumulated stocks of timber at Jarrahdale and Mundijong were slowly reduced, there was some lift in prices, and hope began to dawn.

After the Slump – The Late 'Thirties

By the end of 1934, it was apparent that the Company had successfully weathered the storm, although it had reduced its capital substantially in the process, and orders were once again being received for fresh supplies of timber, both locally and overseas. It was therefore decided that, after all, the big mills at Jarrahdale should be re-opened, and in November 1935,[lxv] after five years of silence, No. 2 mill was re-opened, and the saws began to turn once more. There was also new management, as F. L. ("Tim") Brady retired after twenty-eight years as manager at Jarrahdale.

Alfred Cook – Manager, 1935-1958

The new manager was Alfred Cook, who was transferred from Barton's Mill on the Canning to take over at Jarrahdale. He was a man of wide experience having been engaged in the industry since 1902, his first position being at the old Canning Mill in that year, and in the intervening years had held various positions at many mills. Jarrahdale was fortunate in its new manager, whose duty it was to steer a difficult and successful course in the troubled waters of the coming years when there were many changes, both in the technical methods employed and in the way of life at Jarrahdale.

Ever since the Twenties, the coming of the motor car and truck brought changes in the former way of life. With easy and rapid means of transport the community became less self-contained, a trend which was reinforced by the coming of the "wireless". At the same time the new and easy means of transport enabled bush-workers to live in at the mill town once again, and therefore the old "bush-camps" ceased to be needed, and gradually became just memories of the past. Another innovation brought a great change in the bush workings, leading to the disappearance of the picturesque horse teams.

The Coming of the Tractors

Just as the slow-moving bullocks had given place to the horse teams, so now these, too, gave place to the new mechanical monster, the "crawler" logging tractor. The first of these appeared at Jarrahdale in 1935, the big "Steam Haulers" of the earlier years having been taken out of service. The first tractors imported by the Company were 30 h.p. "Holts", which were first tried out at Yarloop, in 1926 and onwards. These early machines were experimental and did not replace the horse teams to any extent until the middle "Thirties, when the American "Caterpillar" tractors were introduced. These used diesel-fuel, whilst the earlier "Holts" had used petrol.

Soon after the mill re-opened in 1935 the early "Holts" were employed for a time,[lvi] being replaced by "Caterpillars" soon afterwards. It is interesting to note that these early "Caterpillars" cost, in the mid-thirties, about £1,250, but were quite expensive to maintain. Gradually the Company built up a fleet of over 50 of these machines, each model being larger and more powerful than the last — and more costly.

Most of the major repair work was done at Yarloop, machines from Jarrahdale and other of the Company's mills being sent there for the work. Here the Company had an elaborate Tractor Maintenance Workshop in the charge of "Bob" Springthorpe, a highly capable diesel engineer, who had come out from England in the late 'Twenties especially for the work. He was a familiar figure at Jarrahdale, especially as he later became the Engineer Superintendent for all the Company's mills and did not retire until 1968.

Gradually tractors took over from the horse teams, until by 1945 these, together with the giant whims, had disappeared.

Another great change in the bush workings came with the introduction of log-hauling trucks. The first light motor trucks appeared in the 'Twenties but these, although much used for carting sleepers or for the light haulage generally, could not cope with a heavy load of logs. By 1935, when Jarrahdale re-opened, heavier, and more rugged trucks were available, and for three years – up to 1938 – log hauling by motor trucks was tried out, under contract, the contractor being W. Schulstad. After this experiment the contract work was discontinued, log hauling being carried out by tractors only. Three of these, Holts, worked in the bush, hauling trailers on which logs were loaded. Two more tractors, working without trailers, pulled the logs for up to two miles to the bush log-landing, where they were loaded onto railway trucks and hauled into the mill.

So, the 'Thirties passed, with Jarrahdale as prosperous as ever, but it was never quite the same as in pre-depression days. There was always the fear that another 'slump' might come at any time; the old feeling of security had gone. Yet the "slump' did not return; what came was another war, in 1939. Again, Jarrahdale was fortunate, as the mills did not close; the internal demand for timber continued and once again Jarrahdale was very conveniently placed to the greatest market. True, shipments once more fell off, as they had in 1914-18, but the slack was taken up by local demand. As in the previous war, some Jarrahdale men went into the Army, Navy or Air Force, but otherwise, life went on much as before.

The next disaster was not due to closed mills and unemployment nor to the effects of war. This time it was fire.

No.2 Mill Burnt Again

On 4th November 1943, No. 2 mill was destroyed by fire, this being the fifth of Jarrahdale's mills to suffer this fate. The earlier ones were No. 1 (the original mill) in 1895, the re-built No. 1 in 1901, No. 6 in 1910 and No. 2 in 1920, nor was this fire to be the last in the history of the township.

Sawmill fires were terrible things, especially in the days of wooden mill sheds with lines of shafting and inflammable belting. The powder-dry sawdust lies in every crack and on every beam and joist, while the oily, sawdust-covered belting carries the flame to every part of the structure with lightning speed. Sometimes – often – witnesses say the mill "seemed to explode" – and so it was with Jarrahdale's No. 2.

No time was lost in erecting a new mill as described below and production was resumed without delay. However, it was not long before the fire demon struck again.

No. 1 Mill Burnt

"No. 1 Mill", the famous mill which had been built in 1912-13, was not reopened in 1935, after the depression when "No.2" started again, but remained semi-derelict for many years, being cannibalised, the main engine and the "Symondson Log Turner" being sent to a new mill at Quinninup, near Manjimup in the Karri country, while other parts, including most of the roofing, were sent elsewhere. In 1943, when "No. 2" was burnt as mentioned above, a mill was built to take its place on the site of the former "No. 1", this becoming, in fact, the fourth "No.1".

On 19th August 1949 this mill was also destroyed by fire, but was at once rebuilt, the FIFTH "No. 1" mill at Jarrahdale, it still stands today, unused and in a dismantled state.

Of the burning of No. 2 mill, Mr. Cook, the then manager, tells an interesting story.[lxvii] After the fire, two well-known sawmillers, Jack Lewis and Fred Stirk, who jointly owned and operated a mill at Kirup, came to Jarrahdale to see the destruction. Whilst surveying the dismal, blackened scene, Stirk turned to Lewis and said, "You burnt a mill down once, didn't you, Jack?" to which Lewis replied, "Yes, I burnt a mill down." Curious, the manager, Alf Cook, enquired, "What mill was that?"; Lewis replied, "Why, a mill here at Jarrahdale," and went on to explain that at the time he was a lad working in the mill, and one day, when "greasing up" underneath the mill, using a "slush lamp" for light, he got a second slush lamp and tried to light one from the other, and in so doing spilled burning oil into the sawdust down below. The sawdust, being dry and powdery, burst into flame, which being hard to get at spread until the whole mill was destroyed. This mill would have been the second "No. 1" which was destroyed in 1895, when Lewis was about 15 years old. In addition, the mill in question is noted as being 'very old with a shingle roof' suggesting that it was very likely the original No. 1 mill, built in 1872.

After the fire of 1943 and after the new mill was built, it was found that the distance over which logs had to be hauled in some areas was too great for tractors only, so the Company purchased several heavy-duty petrol-driven "White" trucks, eventually having four of these vehicles in use from 1944/45 onwards.[lxviii] Heavy log-hauling trucks now came into general use, being used to work with tractors and to supplement and eventually to entirely replace the bush railways. By 1970 the railways had long gone, being replaced by a fleet of great trucks. The trucks had a great advantage over the railways owing to their flexibility. Log-hauling roads, although expensive to build and maintain, could reach out in any direction, and could readily be put in, and the routes varied as the areas being logged changed, whereas the putting down and pulling up of railway lines was a slow and costly business. Railway lines once down stayed down for a very long time, thus restricting the area in which trees could be economically felled and transported to the mill.

It was at this time, 1950, that the railway line from Mundijong to Rockingham was at last pulled up, some of the rails being purchased for use as lamp standards for the Bunbury trotting ground, although they were then over 70 years old.

Power Saws First Appear in the Bush

It was in the late 'Forties that the first "Power Saws" came on the scene. There were several types, the earlier ones being merely a mobile circular or cross-cut saw, driven by a petrol or deisoline engine and mounted on a wheeled carriage. There was a good deal of experimentation, some of which was carried out at Jarrahdale in 1950, but by the mid-'Fifties, hand-falling had practically ceased. When, in the 1960s, the power chainsaw was introduced, the revolution in the bush was complete. Instead of railways, the motor truck and tractor did the work. Instead of the axe and saw wielded by hand, the power saw brought down the tall trees in a fraction of the time. Above all, there was no longer any need for "bush camps", as the motor car or truck took the workers in the bush to and from their work each day.

Firewood

From the day when the South-West railway line was opened in 1893 Jarrahdale enjoyed a lucrative market for firewood, sold in the metropolitan area of Perth, and, in this, the mills there had a great advantage over competitors, the haul being so short. Vast heaps of firewood soon appeared, particularly at No. 5 mill in the early 1900s. Later, a vast dump arose at Mundijong, and later still, in the 'Fifties, when the Mundijong yard was closed, firewood was stacked beside the new No. 1 and No. 2 mills at Jarrahdale itself. Some of this wood was green "mill-ends" produced every day from waste timber at the mills and sold green, some of it was mill-ends left for drying, and therefore sold at a higher rate, owing to the reduced weight. For years truck after truck of firewood was railed daily to Perth, and, until the 'forties, also to Rockingham. In the" Fifties, it became profitable to despatch this firewood by motor truck and this, although a declining trade, continued for years.

As, in 1950, the railway line from Mundijong to Rockingham was pulled up, no more firewood came there from Jarrahdale, and this link between the forest and the sea ended, to be replaced with a different line and a very different freight in the next decade.

The "Jubilee" Celebrations of 1951

When 80 years had passed since the Wanliss brothers had started building their first mill and the first houses at what was to become the Jarrahdale township, it was decided to hold a "Jubilee Celebration Week". The function was on a big scale, lasting from 27th October to 3rd November 1951.

Entertainments of various kinds were held every day and on most evenings. They included a "Morning and Afternoon Picnic", Sports, Children's Sports, foot-racing and, of course, Log Chopping. The "Celebration" was held under the auspices of the Serpentine-Jarrahdale Road Board (whose first office was at Jarrahdale), with the Chairman of the Board, D. G. Watkins, as President of the organising committee, which included the Manager of Jarrahdale, Alfred Cook and the Jarrahdale Post-Master, Don Glover. The Premier of the State, Mr. Ross McLarty, attended, as well as the Secretary of Millars Timber and Trading Company Ltd., Mr. A. H. Christian, who later became the Chairman of Directors of that company, retiring in 1971. It was a great week for the residents of Jarrahdale, who felt that the clouds of war had now finally passed away, and that a fresh period of prosperity was at hand, as indeed it was.

Throughout the 'Fifties work went steadily on. The bush workings became further and further away from the township. The big motor trucks were steadily taking over from the railways and at one time were hauling logs from a bush area well to the east of the Albany Road and yet, so great had been the growth of the smaller trees not touched in the earlier days, that at times the fallers were working in previously cut-over areas in sight of the township, as they had done away back in the 1870s. By now the power-saws were everywhere in use and the bush camps had long vanished.

The Serpentine Dam

Soon another activity took place not many miles away, when starting in 1957 and finishing in 1961, a huge dam was built in the Serpentine River, to create yet another source of water supply for the metropolitan and nearby rural areas. A truly great work this, and many visitors drove through Jarrahdale to see the work in progress and to admire its beauty when completed. As the waters built up, they covered and drowned the sites of the former No. 5 and No. 6 sawmills, which had been a scene of life and activity from the 1890s until around 1913. When the work was done and the surrounding areas made beautiful with lawns, shrubs, and ornamental trees, the "Serpentine Dam" became one of the favourite tourist attractions near the city of Perth, and visitors came in droves – and still come – to picnic on its banks.

Jarrahdale Has Another New Manager

In 1958 Alfred Cook retired and was replaced by James Bartle, who was transferred from the Company's mill at Mornington. Bartle had been with the Millars' organisation for many years, and before being at Mornington had been the Manager of Hoffman Mill – one of the Yarloop groups – for some time and earlier than this had been with the Company at their major timber depot at Yarloop.

The 'Sixties – And Bauxite

In 1962 James Bartle retired, Tom Linehan being transferred from Quinninup to take over as manager at Jarrahdale. It was in his first year that the last of the old railway line of 1872 – that section which ran from Mundijong to Jarrahdale – was taken over by the West Australian Government Railways and altered to allow for the transport of bauxite ore from the hills around Jarrahdale to the alumina refinery of "Alcoa" at Kwinana, on the shores of Cockburn Sound, thus renewing the contact between the Jarrahdale area and the shipping on the coast. From this time on instead of long rakes of timber trucks towed by steam locomotives puffing their way down to the jetties at Rockingham, great ore-laden steel trucks pulled by big diesel-electric locomotives made their way down to the sea. The route of the old timber line, first surveyed in 1848 and in constant use since 1873, was mainly used, this being re-made with heavier rails. Other sections were completely new. It is unfortunate that beneath where finest jarrah trees stand there also lies the best bauxite ore, with the result that every year about 250 acres of prime timber disappear for good and great machines bite and tear great excavations where once tall timber grew. True, the excavated areas are filled, and re-planting takes place, but not of jarrah, and the success even of this is still an open question. It is sad for Jarrahdale, but perhaps not so for the State of Western Australia, as not only does the bauxite-alumina industry provide work for many people, more so than the sawmills which it robs but also provides a steady export income for the State, as well as royalty payments of around $400,000 per year. Even so, the benefit is an open question, still not fully resolved. To add to Jarrahdale's problems, and that of the timber industry generally is the "die-back" disease, due to a fungus which attacks the root system of the jarrah trees, causing them to "die-back" from the crown, has been a growing problem since the 'Twenties, and Jarrahdale has had its share of trouble. Although the cause of the disease had been known since 1964, the cure is not yet apparent, although it has been checked to a degree. Hence every year wider and wider areas of jarrah forest are killed by the disease, and this, plus the inroads of bauxite mining, steadily reduces the jarrah resources for the future. All these problems the manager at Jarrahdale must face, and in addition, five years after Linehan took over as manager the construction of a new and ultra-modern sawmill was commenced.

The New Mill Built, 1967-68

This mill, which was built half a mile to the east of the previous mill, was equipped with the latest automatic and semi-automatic machinery, thus completing the evolution of sawmilling methods that had been so long in coming. Here electricity has replaced steam power and the long lines of shafting with their belt drives to say bench and docker have gone forever, being replaced with direct electric drive to each machine. No longer do benchmen and tailer-out trudge to and from pushing the heavy timber flitches through the saws. Today the benchman sits at a console, directing and controlling the flow of timber through the mill by a system of electrical controls. For the first time since sawmilling began in the valley, the worker of the 1870s would have no idea how to operate, or even understand, the methods by which the sawn timber he knew so well, flows from the mighty log to the smooth-sawn scantling. It is as well. The old days were hard days.

Today, in 1972, a hundred years after the Wanliss brothers selected a site for their sawmill, many things have changed, but the valley of the Corralong is still beautiful. In the districts surrounding the old town, farms, orchards, and market gardens have appeared, Jarrahdale tomatoes and pumpkins being locally famous. The countryside and even the forest, is always fresh and green around Jarrahdale, as the district enjoys the highest annual rainfall in the South-West of the State. In the period of over 80 years from 1882 to 1963, the annual average was nearly 48 inches – more than 10 inches higher than the metropolitan area of Perth, while in twenty-eight of those years the average was over 50 inches, the record year being 1917 when 85.4 inches of rain were recorded! Visitors and tourists have gradually become more numerous, and today many visitors from every part of Australia and from many countries overseas pass through old Jarrahdale township. Mostly they go straight through on the upper road, to visit the Serpentine Dam, which is a popular place for an afternoon's drive, especially in the Spring and Autumn.

As they go through Jarrahdale, someone in the party may remark ... "This is an old sawmilling town, you know!" and someone else, usually a lady, will remark ... "Look at the funny old houses!" Perhaps a passing glance will be given to the abandoned old sawmill down the valley below, or to where, a little further on, just where the houses in the township end and the road forks toward the Dam they are going to visit, to a great building, obviously quite new, which stands beside the road near the turn-off. The great building could be anything but the popular conception of an old-time sawmill, and visitors do not know that it is not only one of the State's best and most modern sawmills, but is also a direct descendant of the oldest, being the fifteenth in a series of mills which have stood in the valley or in the nearby forest for a hundred years.

They would not know of the immense labour of the pioneers who doggedly dragged the first machinery through the virgin bush to build the first sawmill of 1872, of the "Thomson Steamer" helping with the job and hauling the first logs to the first saws; of the mighty whims with their slow bullocks or glorious eight-horse teams, with their colourful drivers, which came out of the forest and down the track past the old grey weatherboard houses; of the little locomotives, the "Governor Weld", the "Pioneer" with its tall, thin chimney which puffed through the little township for thirty years, or of the "Samsons" No. 1 and No. 2, which were for so many years such a part of Jarrahdale, as they hauled the loaded timber trucks down the hill and over the plain to the waiting sailing ships at Rockingham.

So much has changed. Yet the valley of the Cooralong, with all its history, is just as beautiful as it was in those winter days of 1870 when the Wanliss brothers agreed ... "This is the place for a sawmill."

Afterword

The first of Alcoa's bauxite mines to open in Western Australia was located at Jarrahdale, where mining operations began in July 1963 and continued until rehabilitation of the Langford Park site was completed in May 2001. The mine had ceased production in late 1998.

In 1997 Bunnings closed Jarrahdale's last timber mill, which had been the new 1968 electric mill mentioned on page 95. The closure marked the end of 125 years of timber milling in the town. Some remains of the mill can still be seen.

During the years following the closure of the bauxite mine and timber mills, Jarrahdale has become a mecca for nature-based recreation and tourism. The Bibbulmun Track is a long-distance walking trail from Kalamunda to Albany, 1,003 kms. The track was commissioned in 1979, with the final extension to Albany opening in 1998. It is possible to connect to the Bibbulmun Track from Jarrahdale by either a 15-minute drive to the Sullivan's Rock car park or a four-hour 19.5 km walk via Balmoral Road. The Munda Biddi trail roughly follows the Bibbulmun Track alignment and is a long-distance off-road cycling trail, over 1,000 kms to Albany. The trail opened in April 2013 and passes through Jarrahdale town.

Since 1996 the Jarrahdale Heritage Society has organised regular award-winning bushwalks through the surrounding forests. The walks have gained in popularity, with volunteers maintaining the tracks and opening new areas for visitors to explore. In July 1997, one weekend's hikes through Kitty's Gorge attracted more than 600 people, with Heritage Society volunteers escorting groups of between 50 and 60 walkers. Many of the walks focus on a particular forest theme. In April 2000, a 'Giant jarrah walk' took visitors through the forest to Gooralong Park, where hikers were invited to experience a 'peaceful bushwalk among some of the largest remaining jarrah trees, like those encountered by the first axemen in the 1870s.'

In October 2021, the Shire of Serpentine Jarrahdale endorsed the *Jarrahdale Trail Town Business Case* that had been produced to provide guidance for the Shire in its bid to further Jarrahdale's advancement as one of Western Australia's major trails destinations for visitors seeking equestrian, bushwalking, mountain biking, and heritage trail experiences. By becoming a designated Trail Town, it is envisaged that multiple benefits would flow to both the Jarrahdale community and the broader population. These include economic growth; introducing new business opportunities; improving physical and mental health; and improving environmental awareness and education.

Ron Chapman

V.G. Fall
Courtesy of Judith Fall

About the Author

Victor Fall was born in 1902 in England. As a young boy and encouraged by his father, he developed a lifelong interest in history.

Vic had a high sense of adventure and in 1918, he became an apprentice on a sailing ship, the 'Monkbarns'. After five years at sea, Vic migrated to Australia and took up a clerical position with Millars Timber and Trading Company. He worked at Mornington Mills and Yarloop, and later as an auditor for Millars, visiting many mill towns. During this time, he married and had two children. In WWII, he served with the RAF and was a prisoner of war for three years in Java. Returning to Perth, he worked for several timber companies until his retirement as General Manager of the Swan Timber Company.

Retirement gave Vic the time to focus on his passions of sailing and timber which led to his historical research of the

Western Australian timber industry. While writing 'The Sea and the Forest', a History of Rockingham, he became particularly interested in Jarrahdale, being impressed by its magnificent jarrah forest and the contributions that Jarrahdale had made to the Western Australian timber industry. This culminated in the publication of 'The Mills of Jarrahdale'.

Vic died in 1974 at Shoalwater Bay, Western Australia.

Judith Fall

Appendix 1

The Many Mills of Jarrahdale 1872-1972

No. 1. 1872

The site for the very first mill was selected in 1870 by the Wanliss brothers. It was situated on a small area of level ground, right alongside the Cooralong Brook, just beyond where a ford (now a bridge) crossed the stream. This mill was burnt down and re-built by A. C. Munro when he was relieving manager in 1887. This was the second "No.1" This mill itself was burnt down in 1901 and not re-built at that time. An entirely new "No. 1" was built in 1912-13. This was sited further up the valley. This mill was closed at the start of the depression in December 1929 and did not re-open, being cannibalised, the main engine and the Symondson log turner being sent to Quinninup and some of the roofing sent to other mills, until little of the old mill remained. When No. 2 was burnt in 1943 (see below) another mill was built on the site of the former No. 1. It was re-built "No.1"; was burnt down in 1949, but was re-built. It was abandoned in 1968, when the latest mill was built still further up the valley. There were thus FIVE "No.1s" − NOT including the new mill of 1968.

No. 2 Built in Early 1880s

This mill was situated on the Wongong Brook, about 12 miles from the Jarrahdale township. It was still operating in 1899, but was abandoned soon afterwards, being replaced by another "No. 2" which was built just after "No. 1", was burnt in 1901 (see above). This second "No.2" was burnt in 1920. Yet a third "No.2" was built in 1912-13, at the same time as the new "No.1", the two mills being end-to-end. This latest mill was burnt in 1943. There were thus THREE "No.2s".

No.3. Built about 1890

This was situated on the "39" brook, which flows into the Serpentine River, above the site of the present Serpentine Dam. It was eight miles to the south-east of Jarrahdale and was usually known as "The 39". It was abandoned about ten years later, just before the Amalgamation of 1902.

No.4. Built in the mid-1890s

This mill was also on the Serpentine River, being also about eight miles from Jarrahdale. It was not a big mill, only employing 22 men and four long-hauling teams. It was abandoned at about the same time as No. 3.

No.5. Built in mid 1890s

This mill was originally at "Jarrahglen", fifteen miles to the north-east of Jarrahdale. It was known as "Chandlers", from a farm owned by Chandler in the vicinity. It was later (after 1899) re-built on Big Brook, some ten miles to the south-west of Jarrahdale. The original "Symondson Log Turner" was installed in this mill, being transferred to the New "No.1" in 1913. There were thus TWO "No. 5s"

No. 6 was Built in 1899

This mill was also on Big Brook, ten miles from Jarrahdale. It was burnt down and re-built in 1910. However, it appears to have been abandoned when the new No's 1 and 2 mills were built in 1913.

The Board Mill – Built in 1903-4

This mill was about half-way between No. 5 and No. 6 mills and the Jarrahdale township. It was supplied with timber in flitches sawn at No. 5 and No. 6.

In a century there were thus no less than FIFTEEN sawmills at the Jarrahdale timber station, thus: -

No. 1 Mill built in 1872, 1887, 1912, 1949	5
No. 2 Mill built in 1880s, 1901, 1912/13	3
No. 3 Mill built in 1890 (the "39")	1
No. 4 Mill built in mid 1890s	1
No. 5 Mill built in 1890s (the first "Chandler's, later Big Brook)	2
No. 6 Mill built in 1899, 1910	2
The latest mill, built in 1967/68	1
Total	15

Also, the Board Mill at Jarrahdale, built in 1903-04, and the Board Mill at Mundijong, built in 1918.

No less than six of these mills were destroyed by fire, viz; -

No. 1 in 1887, 1901 and 1949	3
No. 2 in 1920 and 1943	2
No. 6 in 1910*	1
Total	6

A photograph of the re-building of this mill is held in the archives of Millars Timber & Trading Co. Ltd. It is inscribed "No. 6 Mill, Jarrahdale, 1910".

Appendix 2

The Owners of Jarrahdale
1870-1972

Years of Ownership	Name of Owners
1870-1874	Rockingham Jarrah Co. (The Wanliss Company).
1874-1889	Rockingham Jarrah Timber Company
1889-1892	Neil McNeil Co., Jarrahdale Timber Station
1892-1897	Rockingham Railways and Jarrahdale Forests Co.
1897-1902	Jarrahdale Jarrah Forests and Railways Ltd.
1902-1912	Millars' Karri and Jarrah Co. Ltd.
1912-1970	Millars Timber & Trading Co. Ltd.
1970 – onwards	Millars Australia Pty. Ltd.

The Managers of Jarrahdale, 1870-1972

Years in Office	Name	Remarks
1870 to 1876?	Wm. Wanliss	From Ballarat, Vic.
1876 to 1878	Hetherington	Details unknown
1878 to 188?	Steedman	Details unknown
188? to 1887	Ritchie	Was on leave in 1887
1887 (for one year)	A.C. Munro	Relieving Manager
1888 (for a few months)	Michael Kerr	Relieving Manager
1888 (for a few months)	Wm. Atkins	Relieving Manager
1888 to 1893	Ritchie	Returned from leave
1893 to 1907	A.C. Munro	Became Supt. in 1907. Retired 1938. Born in Tasmania in 1858. Died 1950, aged 92.
1907 to 1935	F.L. (Tim) Brady	
1935 to 1958	Alfred Cook	
1958 to 1962	James Bartle	
1962, still in office 1972	Tom Linehan	

The actual sequence of relieving managers in 1888 is not known.

32. P2003.047a G.W.G. Watkins Esq. Chairman of Jarrahdale Road Board, 1902.

33. Council Chambers of the Serpentine-Jarrahdale Shire, at Mundijong, March 1972.

Appendix 3

Some Notable Careers

Jarrahdale is and long has been an ideal place for youth to make a start in life. The air is fresh, the surroundings beautiful with a natural beauty, while good schools have long been available in the valley of the Cooralong.

Beyond the confines of the school life the activities of the outside world; the busy sawmills, the flowing traffic, first by rail and then by road, and, for many years, the coming and going of tall sailing ships at the nearby port of Rockingham. Moreover, the proximity of the capital City of Perth meant that Jarrahdale never suffered from the isolation which was the fate of less fortunate timber towns.

This was particularly true of Jarrahdale at the turn of the century, in the exciting 'Nineties and the early Nineteen-Hundreds, when six sawmills were working in or around the town, and when Rockingham harbour was at the peak of its activity.

Amongst the many young people who grew up at Jarrahdale in those years and who, by ability and hard work, rose to positions of importance and responsibility in later life, a few of the most notable are referred to below.

The Edmondson's. The Edmondson family came to Jarrahdale from York in the very early 1890s, when

Edmondson (Sen.) was appointed Constable-in-Charge of the Jarrahdale Police Station. He had four sons of whom:

Frank, left Jarrahdale when still a child, eventually became the General Manager and Chief Engineer of the State Electricity Commission.

Tom, known as "Slater", Edmondson, entered the Jarrahdale State School in 1894. He had a distinguished career in the Education Department, becoming in due course Acting Director of Education for Western Australia. During the first world war, he served in the A.I.F., being badly wounded at the battle of the Somme.

Jeffery Albert Cousens was the seventh son of Wm. E. Cousens, then the mill carpenter at Jarrahdale. His career provides an excellent example of how a Jarrahdale lad was able to "rise to the top". Jeffery attended the Jarrahdale school at a little later period than Tom Edmondson, and on leaving school commenced duty as a Telegraph Messenger at the Jarrahdale Post Office early in 1913. After qualifying in morse telegraphy he was promoted to Postal Clerk at Williams in 1916, this being soon after five older brothers had left Australia for service in the A.I.G., two of them, Frank and Reubin, being killed in action.

Jeff passed through various channels, and in 1948 was appointed Postal Inspector for the Perth District and acted for lengthy periods as District Inspector at Narrogin, Kalgoorlie, and Bunbury. In 1955 he was selected for the position of Assistant Director for the State of Tasmania, and three years later was elevated to Controller of Post Offices (Australia) with headquarters in Melbourne. After two years he served as Assist. Director, Victoria, and finally for the last three years of approximately fifty-one years in the Postal Department, he returned to Perth as Director for Western

Australia. He retired in 1963, but still maintains a keen interest in Jarrahdale, the town of his boyhood.

W. E. McKenna, O.B.E., J.P. W.E. ("Bill") McKenna was born at Jarrahdale, the son of an old-established Jarrahdale family. He started work with Millars' Karri & Jarrah Co. Ltd. In 1904, as a junior in the Jarrahdale office. Later, he was sent to Karridale, and was the last officer of the Company at Karridale when that Station closed in 1913. Later, in the 'Twenties, he became the manager of Millars' at Bunbury, leaving this position to establish a flourishing Shipping Agency. In 1930 he became the Chairman of the Bunbury Harbour Board, a position he held with distinction until 1966, being honoured on retirement with a well earned O.B.E. He has been for many years a Justice of the Peace at Bunbury, where he is now living in retirement.

The Hanrahan Family. Edward and Mary Hanrahan came to Jarrahdale in 1880. They had a family of five boys and six girls, all of whom did well in later life. They all attended the Jarrahdale school and many of them make their mark in the field of education, no less than seven of them becoming teachers in various schools throughout the State. One daughter, Alice, after starting out as a teacher, changed to a nursing career and for many years was Sister-in-Charge of the St. John of God Hospitals at Subiaco, Belmont, Kalgoorlie, and Geraldton. Undoubtedly this family made a great contribution to the education of youth in the State, and for this their early upbringing at Jarrahdale was certainly responsible.

The Watkins Family. One of the most notable and highly respected families at Jarrahdale and Mundijong was that founded by G.W.G. ("George") Watkins, who, in 1897 took over a property known as the 'Chestnuts' on Location

The Mills of Jarrahdale

105, purchased through auction on 1 December 1858 at £20 per acre to the Batt family. Here a flourishing orchard came into being. George Watkins became a J.P. in 1897 at the early age of twenty-four. He was also one of the earliest Chairmen of the Jarrahdale Road Board, a position later occupied by his son, D.G. ("Glyn") Watkins. Both father and son were, in succession Chairmen of the Jarrahdale Hospital Board.

Mr. D.G. Watkins recalls that the first hospital was opened in a disused stable – hardly the best place for a hospital! The first Resident Medical Officer was Dr. Edward Rommies who commenced practice in 1890. Dr Edwin Ick was RMO at Jarrahdale from January 1902 to September 1904. He owned the first motor car at Jarrahdale – a De Dion. This was in 1899-1900. This hospital was closed in 1957, being replaced by a "Nursing Post". More serious cases then had to go either to Armadale or to Pinjarra. Mr Watkins also remembers the water-powered mill on the Cooralong Brook. This had been built in the 1850s, and it is thought that Joseph Batt who built the flour mill did not come to Serpentine until 1853/54. In the very early days of settlement in the Serpentine district, and the pioneer settlers, whose main diet was kangaroo meat and damper, sometimes bread, used to bring their grain to the mill for grinding into flour. The mill was on a property owned by David Gaffen who was an ex-convict, ticket-of-leave man, who had been transported with a life sentence for rape on what is thought to be questionable evidence, was apparently well respected and served on the Serpentine Jarrahdale Road Board for twelve years. In the 1920s, when an old man, he disappeared and was thought to have been lost in the bush. Although a large police-organised party searched for him for days he was never found.

It is unfortunate that space does not permit the inclusion

of many more Jarrahdale people and families which did so well and made such a contribution to the growth and welfare of the State of Western Australia, but the above few examples show that Jarrahdale has played its part to the full.

Appendix 4

Local Government in the Serpentine Jarrahdale District

Although the Colony of Western Australia, first known as the Swan River Colony, was founded in 1829, it was not until 1871 that steps were taken to set up a system of Local Government. The reason for this was the very small and widely scattered population, which after over forty years had only reached a total of barely 25,000 people. Such roads as existed were mere tracks, most of which had been put in by the settlers themselves.

However, at last, early in 1871 two Acts were passed which laid the foundations of the widespread and efficient system which we know today. These Acts were the Municipalities Act and the Road Districts Act, the latter coming into force in January 1871. This led to the establishment of Roads Boards in districts which had a sufficient population to warrant their creation, but in many areas – of which Serpentine was one – it was a long time before population warranted such a step.

The Serpentine district was first settled as early as the 1840s, the first settler probably being Thomas Peel, who built his "Serpentine Farm" in 1840. This fine property, now known as "Lowlands", afterwards passed into the hands of Wellard and later to the Richardson family, who still own and occupy it. Another early settler was Edward Turner (1831-

1873), who took up a property near the present bridge on the existing South-West highway. Levi Butcher and Baldwin were two other very early settlers in the area.

In the early days of the 1840s and 1850s several settlers took up small ten-acre holdings, and when it was found that the soil in some areas was suitable for fruit trees, orchards appeared, the first being planted by R. Cowan, about 1880, whose orchard was on the corner of the present South-West Highway and Watkins Road. E. Absalom was another early orchardist, while yet another was owned by the Batt family.

A great stimulus was given to the district by the building of the timber railway from Jarrahdale to Rockingham in 1872 as this opened the hill country and provided a small but steady market for produce in the new township of Jarrahdale. Twenty years later an even greater help to the area was the construction of the Government railway in 1893. This linked Bunbury and Pinjarra with Perth and gave farmers in the Serpentine district for the first time a reliable and cheap form of transport to the rapidly growing metropolitan area of Perth, where the influx of immigrants, led by the lure of the new goldfields was rapidly increasing the population.

The new Government railway crossed the line of the "Rockingham Railways and Jarrahdale Forests Company" at a place which came at once to be known as "Jarrahdale Junction", and later as Mundijong. At that time a hotel stood close to the spot where the new Government line crossed the timber company's line, forming an unusual "H" or "Diamond" crossing. The hotel was on land owned by M. Szczecinski, who also owned the hotel. The Government resumed the land for the new railway and Szczecinski built a new hotel which still stands as the "Mundijong Hotel". Szczecinski was a Pole and was an excellent carpenter and joiner. The stairway and banisters of his new hotel, fine pieces of work, were built by him.

The first hotel in the area was at Whitby Falls. E.D. Cockram, a pioneer landowner, was the licensee.

One major effect of the new railway line was that the Jarrahdale timber company set up a timber stacking yard at Jarrahdale Junction, shortly afterwards establishing a timber dressing mill. This depot remained for over sixty years, becoming one of the largest in the State.

It is interesting to note that from 1893 to 1898 the Jarrahdale Junction township was listed in the W.A. Post Office Directory under the heading of "Jarrahdale", but that from 1899 onwards the listing became "Mundijong" with Jarrahdale residents being shown under that heading, a clear indication of the growing size and importance of the Mundijong township. Already, by 1895, it had a Post Office, with Mrs. Kiernan listed as "Postmistress".

By the late 1890s, the population of the Serpentine-Jarrahdale district had grown sufficiently large to warrant the formation of a Road Board, and in December 1896 a Road District was created, known as the "Serpentine Road District". The boundary of the district extended from the seacoast on the south-west corner of the Rockingham townsite and ran eastwards as far as the Perth-Albany Road, thus including Jarrahdale; the southern boundary ran parallel with, and about 920 chains south of the northern boundary, with the Perth-Albany Road as the eastern boundary.

It is of interest to note that the neighbouring Rockingham Road District was created at about the same time, the Rockingham Roads Board holding its first meeting in May 1897.

The first members of the Serpentine Road Board were:

                Mr. N. Anstey – Chairman
Messrs. N.J. Butcher
            R. Cowan
            W. Butcher
            R. Tonkin
            N.J. Turner

The first financial statement issued by the Board was published in the Government Gazette of 28th October 1898, and this showed that the sole source of the Board's income for the year 1897 was a government grant totalling £450. In those happy days there was no rate levy! The bulk of the grant was expended on the construction of what was then known as the "Jarrahdale Main Road".

The Board operated until May 1902, when an area which consisted of that portion of the district east of the Perth-Bunbury Road, was excised from the Serpentine Road Board, and was constituted as the "Jarrahdale Road District".

The first members of this Board were:

                Mr. E.H. Absalom – Chairman
Messrs. G.W.G. Watkins
            A.C. Munro
            H.J. Butcher
            H. Firim
            W. Baldwin.

The Secretary was John Adamson, part-time at £12 per annum.

The second Chairman, 1902-1913 was G.W.G. Watkins.

The first office of the Jarrahdale Road Board was a small timber-framed weatherboard building built between the Cooralong Brook and the railway line, at the eastern end of

The Mills of Jarrahdale

the No. 1 sawmill. It was replaced by a new office built one chain east of the Post Office, almost opposite the company's former "Cottage". It was a very small building of one room only, 12ft. x 10ft.

Not only was Mr. G.W.G. Watkins the second Chairman of the Jarrahdale Road Board, but in later years from 1945 onwards, his son Mr. D.G. ("Glyn") Watkins was Chairman of the later Serpentine-Jarrahdale Road Board, father and son thus giving between them no less than sixty years of service to local government in the Serpentine-Jarrahdale district.

The two separate Boards operated until August 1913, when a portion of the area was transferred to the Rockingham Road District, and the remainder, which was in fact a reunion of the Serpentine and Jarrahdale Districts, became the Serpentine-Jarrahdale District, as it still is today.

It was in this year, 1913, that Jarrahdale was first gazetted as a "township"[7] although it had already been in existence for over forty years.

The report covering the operations of the new Board for the year ended June 1914, the first year of operation, gives the following information:

Rates Collected	£ 686 16 0
Cart and Carriage Licences	£ 63 15 0
Dog Licences	£ 14 10 0
Motor Car Licences	£ 7 0 0
Other Licences	£ 4 0 0
Government Grants	£ 419 0 0
All other receipts	£ 5 11 3
	£1200 12 3

---

[7] Government Gazette 11/7/1913

It is interesting to see that the Government Grant still made up a great part of the Board's revenue, and that, even in 1914, there was at least one motor car to license.

The first office was a timber building at Mundijong. This was demolished in 1949, when new offices were built on the same site, adjacent to the Memorial Hall. The Chairman at that time was Mr. D.G. Watkins, who held office until his retirement in 1952. These offices were occupied until March 1972 when new and up-to-date offices were opened, not far from the previous building.

Apart from minor boundary adjustments with neighbouring Boards, the Serpentine-Jarrahdale Road District operated until July 1961, when it became the "Shire of Serpentine-Jarrahdale".

The present members of the Serpentine-Jarrahdale Shire Council are:

President – H.C. Kentish
Deputy President – F. Senior
Councillors: Messrs. L.G. Atwell
L.M. Muller
J.M. Oliver
L.H. Fawcett
G.C. Brickwood

Jarrahdale Junction was re-named Mundijong when a township was declared in 1893. Four years later, in 1897, the first Mundijong State School was opened. By the mid-1920s Mundijong was a very busy railway centre, and it is recorded that in 1925, 30,184 tons of local timber and 12,355 tons of firewood were forwarded from the station. Other items forwarded in that year were 104 tons of fruit, 210 cattle, 29 calves, 585 pigs, 47 horses and 3,640 sheep, as well as 2,585 tons of other classes of goods. In addition, 13,822 passenger journeys were booked.

Mundijong has come a very long way since the time of the early pioneers. Prior to 1951, the greater part of the revenue of the Serpentine-Jarrahdale Road Board was drawn from the Jarrahdale portion of the district, but since that date the position has been reversed, and the Mundijong area became the major source of revenue. In recent years, however, Jarrahdale, Serpentine and Keysbrook have been the scene of vigorous orchard and market gardening development, Jarrahdale's tomatoes and pumpkins finding a good and growing market. At the same time, the commencement of bauxite mining in the Jarrahdale Forest area has created yet another activity, while the long-established timber industry can still look forward to very many years of life.

Notes and References
Books and Documents Consulted

Kimberley, W.B.: "History of West Australia: a narrative of her past together with biographies of her leading men", compiled by W.B. Kimberley. Published by F.W. Niven & Company. Melbourne and Ballarat. 1897.

Colebatch, Sir Hal (Editor): "A Story of a Hundred Years": Western Australia, 1829-1929. Edited by Sir Hal Colebatch, C.M.G., Perth Government Printer, 1929.

Hammond, J.E.: "Western Pioneers – The Battle Well Fought". Edited by Osland K. Battye. Printed and published by Imperial Printing Company Limited, Perth. 1936.

Lukis, M.: "A History of Rockingham". Typescript in Battye Library: two papers, both Ref. PR 638.

Robertson, J.R.: "A History of the Timber Industry in Western Australia". Held in Battye Library. A very able and comprehensive study of the industry, from the earliest days of the Colony up to 1956. (Note: The Robertson family lived for many years at Jarrahdale.)

Thomas, W.C.: A series of articles published in the "Australian Timber Journal". Sydney, N.S.W. 1938 and in the "Western Mail", Perth, W.A., in March and April 1939. The notes sited below refer to the "Western Mail". Held in Battye Library.

Martin James: "A Short Description of a visit to the Company's Mills and Forests", being a report to the shareholders of the "Jarrahdale Jarrah Forests and Railways Ltd." Company. In brochure form: dated "London 1899": Typescript copy in Battye Library: Ref. PR 6248.

Endnotes:

[i] Kimberley, p 44
[ii] Ibid, p 58
[iii] Ibid, p 63
[iv] Ibid, p 63
[v] Ibid, p 45
[vi] Ibid. p 131
[vii] Ibid. p 102
[viii] Robertson, p 2
[ix] Letter in possession of Mrs H. Richardson, of "Lowlands", Mardella.
[x] Robertson, p 4
[xi] Boyce. P. J. "Governors of Western Australia". Thesis. University of Western Australia. University studies in History. Vol. 4. Battye Library.
[xii] Robertson, p 8
[xiii] Robertson, p 7
[xiv] S.F., Ch 5
[xv] Hammond, p 7
[xvi] S.F., Ch 5
[xvii] ibid
[xviii] Colebatch, p 6
[xix] Robertson, p 7
[xx] S.F., Ch 5
[xxi] Information from Alfred Cook of Rockingham and the late Chas. Siford of Jarrahdale.
[xxii] ibid
[xxiii] James Martin
[xxiv] Fremantle Shipping Register, 1873 (Battye Library).
[xxv] Hammond, p 24
[xxvi] S.F., Ch 5
[xxvii] Hammond, p 23

[xxviii] Information from Mr. D.G. Watkins, formerly Chairman of the Jarrahdale Roads Board.

[xxix] Information from Sgt. Rule, who was constable at Jarrahdale at the time of the move.

[xxx] Royal W.A. Historical Society Journal Vol. IV. Part 2, 1950. Article "The memories of Mrs. Phoebe Christie".

[xxxi] "Notes on the Timbers of Western Australia", issued under the authority of the Hon. J. Newton Moore, Minister for Land and Agriculture. Perth, Government Printer. 1906.

[xxxii] Thomas, Article 9, "R.O. Law" 18/4/39.

[xxxiii] Woodland, E.W. Article in the "Australian Railway Historical Society," Bulletin 356, June 1967; Locomotives "Samson", No. 1 and No. 2.

[xxxiv] Robertson, p 16

[xxxv] Thomas, Article 7, "A.C. Munro", 18/4/39

[xxxvi] Robertson, p 16

[xxxvii] Woodland, op. cit.

[xxxviii] Thomas, Article 7, op. cit.

[xxxix] S.F., Ch 5

[xl] James Martin, op. cit.

[xli] S.F., Ch 5

[xlii] Post Office Directory ("Wises") 1894-1900.

[xliii] M. Lukis, op. cit. Also see references to locomotives in James Martin.

[xliv] S.F., Ch 5

[xlv] ibid

[xlvi] ibid

[xlvii] Information from Alfred Cook, Rockingham

[xlviii] S.F., Ch 5

[xlix] Information from Alfred Cook, Rockingham

[l] ibid

[li] S.F., Ch 5

[lii] ibid

[liii] ibid

[liv] Information from Alfred Cook. Rockingham.
[lv] Woodland, op. cit.
[lvi] Information from George Dare of Eaton.
[lvii] Information from g. Gilbride and the late Charles Siford, both of Jarrahdale.
[lviii] Robertson, p 333. Also see Thomas, Article 15, 27/4/39
[lix] Information from Alfred Cook, Rockingham.
[lx] Information from Mrs. A. Bradshaw, a granddaughter of Mrs. Cope.
[lxi] For a detailed study of the strike see "The W.A. Timber Workers' Strike of 1907": dissertation submitted by Bro. R.F. Keane for the Degree of B.A. with Honours: Dept. of History, University of Western Australia, May 1971.
[lxii] In 1909
[lxiii] Thomas, Article 15, "Amalgamation", 27/4/39
[lxiv] "West Australian", Article "Jarrahdale Revives", November 1935
[lxv] ibid
[lxvi] Information from Alfred Cook, Rockingham.
[lxvii] ibid
[lxviii] Ibid

www.ingramcontent.com/pod-product-compliance
Lightning Source LLC
Chambersburg PA
CBHW021153080526
44588CB00008B/322